A COMPLETE GUIDE TO EXPLORING THE CAPITAL FOR FAMILIES

London With Kids

BY KATJA GASKELL AND CATHY WINSTON

Copyright © 2025 by Katja Gaskell and Cathy Winston
All rights reserved.
No portion of this book may be reproduced in any form without written permission from the publisher or author, except as permitted by UK copyright law.

For Alfie, Tess, Sam and Sylvia
who always make exploring London fun

London with Kids: Contents

OVERVIEW

Welcome to London	12
Money saving tips	14
How to get around London	16
Getting into London from the airports	19

ITINERARY IDEAS

How to spend 1 to 7 days in London	23

THEMED ITINERARIES

Welcome to Roman Londinium	44
Fashion forward	47
Please look after this bear!	50
London's burning!	53
Get sporty	55
Thrills and spills	59
Wizarding fun	62

THINGS TO DO

10 Umissable things to do in London	66
10 Hidden gems in London	68
Best day trips from London	71
London's best views	78
London's great outdoors	80

LONDONWITHKIDS.COM | 7

WHERE TO EAT

Best family restaurants	84
Best places for treats	86

WHERE TO STAY

Best family hotels	90
Best budget hotels	91
Best mid-range hotels	92
Best luxury hotels	93
Best hotels sleeping 5	94
Best hotels with pools	95

LONDON ESSENTIALS

Festivals & events	98
Don't go home without…	101
Packing checklist	102

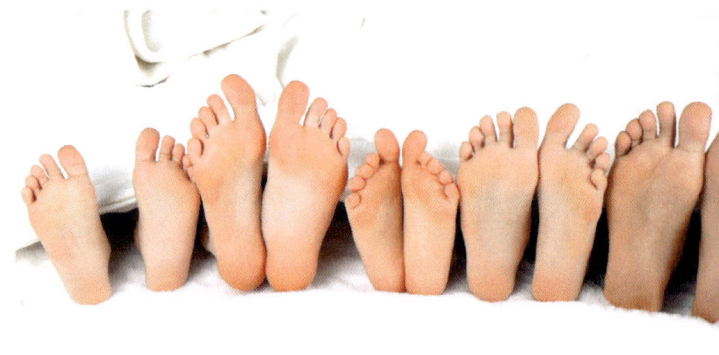

Meet Katja & Cathy

Hello and welcome to London with Kids. We are Katja and Cathy, two journalists, family travel bloggers and local Londoners who love to explore everything the city has to offer.

We have four children between us and know what it's like to navigate the city with everyone from babies to toddlers to teens.

This book is the result of the London with Kids Facebook group that we launched in early 2020, just before the pandemic hit and travel ground to a halt.

When the world started to reopen, the group's numbers grew rapidly with hundreds of new member requests daily. The group - along with Katja and Cathy's own family travel blogs - aims to answer any and all questions visitors and locals have about travelling to London with their own kids, from the best places to stay and how to save money to the all-important questions of finding the city's top ice cream and desserts.

London can appear overwhelming and planning a trip can seem impossible but we promise you that it's not! This guide will arm you with all the information you need (in easy-to-digest chapters) to make it as simple as possible for you to plan the perfect visit to London with kids.

Enjoy!

Katja & Cathy

Welcome to London!

We love London and are of the firm belief that this is one of the best cities in the world for families. But London is also a very big city and planning a family trip to the capital can feel overwhelming.
This guide has been designed to not only help you navigate your way around the city but to ensure that everyone has a great time too.
To get you started, here are some tips.

LONDON IS A BIG CITY

It might seem an obvious thing to say but London is a *big* city. Sights, attractions and events are spread across the city meaning that there is no one central area that is best placed for seeing everything. Check your map when looking at places to stay.

THE TRANSPORT NETWORK IS EXCELLENT

Londoners might like to moan about the Underground (and rush hour on the Northern Line is no fun) but we do know how lucky we are to have such an efficient public transport system. Extensive and easy to use, the **Transport for London** network is first class.

PLAN YOUR BUDGET

London can be an expensive city but there are ways to keep costs down (read on for more). If you visit at peak times, expect hotel prices in particular to rise. Popular times include the school half term breaks (typically end of October, mid-February and late May), bank holidays, Christmas, Easter, and the summer months. You can save money by visiting during the shoulder seasons.

STAND ON THE RIGHT

Want to blend in? Always (and we mean, always!) stand on the right-hand side of the escalator, especially when travelling by tube.

LONDON'S WEATHER IS...

...entirely unpredictable! You may enjoy sunshine and blue skies one day and heavy rains and wind the next, no matter the time of year. Pack layers and an umbrella.

PLAN AHEAD

It's impossible to see everything that London has to offer in one trip (or even one lifetime) so it pays to spend some time planning your stay. If visiting during high season, do book tickets to popular attractions in advance. This guide offers itinerary ideas and suggestions. London with Kids also offers a bespoke **trip planning service.**

PLUG IN

London uses a type-G plug. If travelling from overseas, make sure you buy an adaptor before arriving in London.

CHECK YOUR CREDIT

London is largely cashless these days so make sure you have a credit card that has a chip and a 4-digit PIN. Double-check whether your card offers free foreign transactions.

TIPPING

Tipping is not expected in London. Most restaurants will add a certain percentage - typically 10 to 15% - to your bill as a service charge that goes towards the staff.

GET WALKING

London is a very walkable city. Yes, it's big but it's also very easy to navigate on two feet, and walking is sometimes faster than taking the tube, especially if your destination is only a couple of stops away.

LONDONWITHKIDS.COM | 13

Money Saving Tips

London is a brilliant city for families but it can be expensive. Here's how to make your money go further.

DISCOUNT TICKET WEBSITES

Wowcher is good for short-term deals. Find everything from reductions on **London bus and boat tours** to packages including a hotel and theatre tickets. **Tiqets** specialises in discounts on attractions. **Piqniq** has regular deals on family attractions too.

TKTS London and **Todaytix** are great for theatre discounts.

BLUE PETER BADGES

Blue Peter badge holders can visit **200 places in the UK** for free, including London Zoo, the Tower of London and HMS Belfast. Blue Peter is a popular **UK children's television show** and badges are awarded to those appearing on the show or by sending a creative contribution.

KELLOGGS DEALS

With regular deals on cereal and snack packs, you can often get one adult ticket free for **Merlin attractions** if you buy another adult or child ticket full price.

KIDS PASS

With up to 57% off on days out and attractions, as well as deals on restaurants, the **Kids Pass** could save you a bundle. There is a monthly and annual membership options. A 30 day trial costs £1.

NATIONAL RAIL

The long-running **National Rail 2 for 1 deal** covers a string of London attractions, including **London Zoo**, if you have a valid train ticket.

14 | LONDONWITHKIDS.COM

FREE THINGS TO DO

There are also LOTS of free things to do in London. Some of our top picks are:

- **London Museums:** Many are free including some of the biggest and most popular, such as the Natural History Museum, the Science Museum and the British Museum.
- **Sky Garden:** See the London skyline for free at the city's highest public garden.
- **Playgrounds:** London has some incredible spaces to play and they are all free!
- **Ceremony of the Keys:** A centuries old tradition performed at the Tower of London (advance booking essential, £5 admin charge for tickets).
- **Splash Parks:** Cool down for free at one of the city's many splash parks.
- **Kids Eat Free:** During school holidays some restaurants offer a 'kids eat free' deal.

DISCOUNT THEATRE SITES

Various websites offer deals on London Theatre Shows including **TKTS London** (there's also a TKTS booth in Leicester Square) and **Todaytix**. Kids Week runs throughout August with great discounts.

LONDON CITY PASSES

The **London Pass** includes entry to over 90 attractions and is valid on consecutive days for between 1 and 7 days (plus a 10 day option).

The **London: Go City Explorer Pass** gives access to over 100 attractions, valid for 60 days after your first visit.

LONDONWITHKIDS.COM | 15

London's public transport system may appear overwhelming but you'll find that using the tube, and the rest of the Transport for London (TfL) network (buses, Elizabeth line, DLR and the overground rail lines) is actually a lot simpler than you might think.

WHAT YOU NEED TO KNOW

The underground is divided into **six main zones** that continue out in concentric circles from the middle. Most visitors will spend their time in the most central **zone 1**.

You don't need to pay much attention to which zones you're visiting. If you're using **contactless payment**, you'll automatically be charged based on the stations you visit (which is why you must always tap in and out on the yellow pads at the entry/exit gates) with a max daily/weekly cap.

Oyster cards work the same way, just make sure you load enough credit. It's only the old-style **paper travelcards** where you need to specify which zones you're visiting (avoid these though as they are more expensive).

Each **tube line** has a **different colour** so you needn't learn all the names, you can simply look for the shade you need. Even the two shades of blue – light blue for the Victoria line and dark blue for the Piccadilly line – are easy to tell apart.

There are **maps everywhere** around tube stations. Along with maps as you go in to the station, you'll find details for each individual line as you approach the platforms – so if you aren't sure if you're going northbound or southbound, it isn't a problem, simply look for your station.

There are also more **maps on the platforms** themselves, so you can doublecheck you're in the right place, and plenty of signs directing you if you need to change lines.

If you're not sure where to go when you get off a tube train, move straight over to the wall and wait for the crowds to leave so you can work it out without blocking the platform.

Electronic signs on the platform will tell you when the next train is due. They're listed by the station where they terminate – usually this is the **end of the line**, although some trains will stop part-way along the line.

Some lines split, including the **Northern**, **Piccadilly** and **District Lines**, so make sure you take the right branch.

There's **rarely a long wait** between trains except at night, although you may need to wait a little longer on Sundays. If there are problems on the line, there will be notifications and signs telling you of delays as you enter, so you can make alternative plans if you need to.

Be prepared for **stairs and long walks** in some stations. Although many tube stations have **escalators**, some of the older ones or those further out of the centre will also have stairs to navigate.

A limited number of stations will have **lifts/elevators**. You can see these marked with **'step-free access'** on tube maps.

And **always stand on the right** of escalators unless you're walking up/down.

LONDONWITHKIDS.COM | 17

KIDS TRAVEL FREE

Good news if you have **children aged under 11**, as they travel free on the TfL network - including the Underground (aka the tube), buses, the DLR and Elizabeth Line. Simply take younger kids with you through the wide/luggage gates in stations, rather than the individual gates.

Remember that this only applies to public transport in London and doesn't apply to national and regional trains, where only kids under 5 go free.

TEENS/TWEENS GET 50% OFF

Children aged 11-15 pay half-price on Tfl services - buy an Oyster card for £7 and ask Tfl staff to add the **Young Visitor discount.**

HOW TO GET AROUND

There are some very **useful apps** to help you navigate London's public transport.

Citymapper is one of the best: simply add in the start and end location of your journey, plus when you want to travel, and it will give you a choice of different routes using bus, tube, taxi and even bicycle. If travelling by London Underground, It may even tell you which tube carriage is best for a speedy exit.

Tfl Go is another handy one, while **Google Maps** has real-time information for buses.

Getting into London from the Airports

London is well served with airports, with five close to the city, including four of the UK's five busiest airports. Only two are on the TfL network, so you may have to take a train or coach to get to central London but transport links are good.

Taxis and airport transfers are another option but they're often slower, thanks to traffic, and always more expensive. Driving in central London is also best avoided, with various charges in force as well as pricy parking.

In most cases, it's cheaper to buy tickets in advance, although you can use contactless or Oyster cards on many rail services as well as the TfL network. Each rail company has its own booking site, but you can also use websites like TheTrainline.com and Omio.co.uk for National Rail services.

HEATHROW

The biggest airport in both the UK and Europe, there are several different options to get from Heathrow to central London.

Take the tube – the cheapest option is via the Piccadilly line on the London Underground, with separate stops for the different terminals.

Elizabeth line – faster, air-conditioned and more spacious, the latest addition to the tube network also runs from Heathrow into central London but costs slightly more than standard tube fares.

Heathrow Express trains – the fastest way to travel from the airport, the trains take 15 minutes non-stop to Paddington. It's also the most expensive public transport option, unless you book well in advance.

Coach - both National Express and Megabus run coaches from Heathrow airport to central London, with the cheapest tickets costing less than tube fares. However, traffic in central London can mean the journey time is longer.

GATWICK

Around 30 miles south of central London, this is the UK's second busiest airport. The airport's station is at the South Terminal, with a free shuttle linking it to the North Terminal.

Southern trains – run from Gatwick to both Victoria and London Bridge stations in central London (stopping at Clapham Junction). It's part of a standard national rail route so can be busier than the Gatwick Express but isn't significantly slower and is often cheaper.

Thameslink trains – run from Gatwick to London Bridge, Blackfriars, Farringdon and St Pancras International (and onward to Luton Airport). Another standard rail route, it can be busy at peak times.

Gatwick Express trains - the dedicated airport trains to Victoria station take around 30 minutes without stopping, with around two running every hour. Designed for passengers with lots of luggage, they're more spacious and don't stop along the way, but fares are usually more expensive.

Coaches - National Express coaches run from Gatwick airport to Victoria in central London, via Heathrow and Hammersmith, departing from both terminals. The journey takes at least two hours 30 minutes to reach central London, and traffic can delay you further.

STANSTED

Served by a string of low-cost airlines, especially Ryanair, Stansted airport is situated north-east of London with routes serving the east of the city.

Trains – the Stansted Express is the only route from Stansted airport to central London. It is the branded airport train operated by Greater Anglia railway, so you can book through either site but it will be the same train and timetable. These run to Liverpool Street Station via Tottenham Hale.

Be aware that there's a separate station nearby called Stansted Mountfitchet, so any tickets should be to/from Stansted airport.

Coaches - there are two coach companies running from Stansted to different stations in central London. **National Express** runs to London Stratford (the quickest route) as well as to Liverpool Street, plus a less frequent route to Victoria coach station via north London.

Airport Bus Express also has coaches to Liverpool Street and Stratford. Bear in mind that traffic in central London can delay all coach journeys.

LONDON CITY AIRPORT

The closest airport to the centre of London, London City airport is also the smallest.

DLR (Docklands Light Railway) – the airport is on the TfL network, with the DLR connecting you to the main tube lines and Elizabeth line. The London City Airport DLR station is in Zone 3.

Bus – TfL buses run from London City Airport. The 473 route runs towards Stratford International, to connect to the tube network, but realistically, the DLR is likely to be the best option for the vast majority of visitors.

LONDON WITH KIDS ITINERARIES

The Main Sights

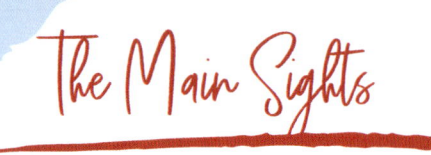

Stroll down **The Mall**, an important ceremonial route dating back to 1660 that runs from Buckingham Palace to Trafalgar Square where you can see the stone lions, ogle Nelson's Column and visit the National Gallery.

Alternatively, head towards **Westminster Abbey** for a peek inside. Tour the Houses of Parliament and snap a picture of Big Ben.

UP HIGH AND ON THE RIVER

It's a short walk from both Trafalgar Square and Big Ben to the **London Eye**, a giant ferris wheel on the banks of the River Thames. Catch a sunset ride around the wheel for a magical bird's-eye view of London's skyline.

Another option is to catch a **City Cruises** tour or **UBER boat by Thames Clippers** and take a trip along the River Thames, which runs through the heart of the city.

TOURS WITH TEA

Brigit's Bakery runs sightseeing tours with afternoon tea on board cherry red Routemaster buses. Themes include Peppa Pig and Paddington, as well as Christmas. See the sights while eating cake.

Want more?

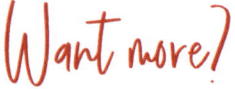

- Go to the Tower of London
- Walk over Tower Bridge
- See 10 Downing Street

Day 2: The Tower of London

MORNING

Start your day at the **Tower of London**, the perfect place to discover almost 1,000 years of history. Dodge the queues by heading straight to the **Crown Jewels**, then set off to explore the rest of the fortress.

It's easy to spend at least **half a day** here: take a look at a medieval king's apartments, see graffiti left by prisoners across the centuries, find armour on display in the ancient **White Tower** and discover the memorial to two Queens executed on the site.

You can also learn about the **royal menagerie of beasts** once housed here and coins made at the **Royal Mint**. Watch out for the **Tower's ravens**; legend says that if they ever leave, the kingdom will fall.

Pick up the Tower's own guidebook for kids or join one of the free tours led by the Yeomen Warders - better known as Beefeaters.

AFTERNOON

Refuel at **Borough Market**, one of the best places in the city for foodies, with a string of stalls selling delicious dishes from around the world, plus some very tempting desserts.

Then head back along **Bankside** towards **Tower Bridge**. Easily the most famous of London's bridges, with its iconic blue and white paint, you can head inside to discover its history – including the story of the bus which jumped from one side to the other.

There are some great views along the Thames from its high-level walkways as well as a chance to peer down through its glass floors, plus a children's trail.

ENJOY MORE VIEWS

Save time to enjoy some more great river views. A 10-minute walk from the Tower, the **Sky Garden** is London's highest public garden. Book **free tickets** in advance. Nearby **Horizon 22** or **Garden at 120** are good alternatives. Or head across the river and up London's tallest building for the **View from the Shard.**

DON'T MISS …

Time your visit right and watch **Tower Bridge lift** to allow river traffic through. The best views on the north bank are near the Tower of London and St Katherine's Pier or find a spot near HMS Belfast or Butler's Wharf on the south bank.

- Take a boat tour
- Visit HMS Belfast
- Follow the Thames path

LONDONWITHKIDS.COM | 27

Day 3: South Kensington

MORNING

South Kensington is home to some of London's best-known museums, and an unmissable location for families. Start at the **Natural History Museum**, home to London's famous dinosaur collection as well as the dramatic blue whale skeleton as you enter.

There are around **80 million items** in the collection altogether (not all on display) covering zoology, paleontology, botany, entomology and mineralogy, in one of London's most eye-catching museum buildings.

Step into an earthquake simulator in the **Red Zone**, check out the mammals collection and look out for the temporary exhibitions too.

Entry is free, except for the temporary exhibitions. Pre-booking is highly recommended, especially in school holidays.

AFTERNOON

You'll find plenty of places to grab lunch, from museum cafes to chain restaurants nearby, or treat yourself to afternoon tea at the **Ampersand Hotel**; themes include Jurassic and Science teas.

Then head to the **Science Museum**, with collections covering science and technology, from the oldest surviving steam locomotive to a model of DNA and the forerunners of computers.

South Kensington

Free to enter (pre-booking recommended), younger kids will love The Garden area in the basement for hands-on fun, as well as the Pattern Pod. The shows and interactive displays at Wonderlab (paid timed tickets) are one of the biggest highlights. Expect to have to tow kids reluctantly out of here!

ROYAL STYLE

Nearby **Kensington Palace** was the childhood home of Queen Victoria, as well as a favourite of George II and his court, and home to Diana, Princess of Wales. Challenge your family to Georgian games, play dress up and discover 19th century scandal.

GET OUTDOORS

Two of the city's royal parks are in walking distance - perfect to combine with museum visits. **Kensington Gardens** stretches for an impressive 265 acres, including one of the city's best play areas, the **Diana Memorial Playground**. Look out for the Peter Pan statue near the Long Water, while kids will also love feeding the green parakeets which flock around the park.

Hyde Park is the second biggest royal park at 350 acres; you'll find the **Diana Memorial Fountain**, Speaker's Corner and the Serpentine Lake .

- Victoria & Albert Museum
- The Royal Albert Hall
- Visit Harrods

30 | LONDONWITHKIDS.COM

Day 4: Covent Garden & Leicester Square

MORNING

Start your day at the **London Transport Museum,** which sits in the old Grade II-listed Flower Market building in **Covent Garden's piazza**. This excellent museum is one of those rare galleries that is just as good for toddlers as it is for tweens, with a wide range of activities for all ages.

The museum explores the **story of London** and its **transport system** over the last 200 years and is filled with old trains, buses, omnibuses and more. There are lots of interactive activities and a fantastic gift shop as well. It's easy to spend **half a day** here.

Entry to the London Transport Museum gives you unlimited return visits for 12 months from the date stated on your ticket. Kids go free!

AFTERNOON

Enjoy lunch in **Seven Dials Market** before walking towards **Leicester Square**, right in the busy heart of tourist London.

Explore **Scenes on the Square** and snap photos with your favourite film characters including Paddington. Head to the giant **LEGO store**, the largest in the world, and be amazed by the many interactive brick sculptures. Opposite is **M&M World**, four floors of brightly coloured sweet treats. **Hamleys Toy Store** is not far away on Regent Street.

Leicester Square is where big blockbuster movie premieres are held. Catch a film at one of the **cinemas** or find cheap theatre tickets at the **TKTS Booth**.

Covent Garden & Leicester Square

DISCOVER CHINATOWN

Located between Covent Garden and Leicester Square, it's Europe's largest **Chinatown**. Gerrard Street runs through the centre lined with buildings and shops decorated with lanterns and dragons. You can't miss the stone lions and Chinese-style gates as you explore the area.

Stop in at **Bun House** for fluffy steamed buns, **Candy Cafe** for 'bubble tea', the **Bubblewrap Dessert Shop** for a bubble waffle, and **Yolkin** for an ice cream sandwich .

DON'T MISS...

Covent Garden has always been a site for **street performers** with the first recorded show – a marionette show – having taken place in 1662. Head to the open square in front of St Paul's Church on the West Piazza and you'll almost always find someone performing.

- See a West End show
- Go shopping - as well as big name shops near the Piazza, Seven Dials is home to fun small boutiques.
- Enjoy an extraordinary ice-cream creation at the Milk Train

LONDONWITHKIDS.COM

Day 5: The South Bank

MORNING

The **South Bank** is unmissable for families - packed with family attractions, it's a great place to stroll along the river, with Instagrammable views and plenty to discover on the way.

Start by soaking up the views from the **London Eye**, the city's iconic observation wheel but then there's lots to do along this stretch of river.

Younger kids will love the **Sea Life London aquarium**, home to 500 species in 14 themed zones. Meanwhile **Shrek's Adventure** transports you to the land of Far Far Away to meet your favourite characters.

For older (and braver!) kids, **The London Dungeon** brings you face to face with London's Great Fire and Sweeney Todd.

AFTERNOON

Save some time for a walk and to check out the events which regularly take place around the **Southbank Centre**, including a food market, Christmas market, and the **Imagine Children's Festival** in February.

London's South Bank stretches from Lambeth Bridge to Blackfriars Bridge before becoming Bankside. It only takes around 30 minutes to walk from the **London Eye** to **Southwark Bridge** to visit the **Tate Modern**, **Shakespeare's Globe**, the **Clink Prison** and the **Golden Hinde**.

Tate Modern is free, with suggested routes for families to follow. There are tours as well as performances at **The Globe**.

The South Bank

FOR SOMETHING DIFFERENT...

There's more than just the big-name attractions:

- Visit the **Leake Street Tunnel** beneath Waterloo station. At 300m long, it's London's longest legal graffiti wall. Take your own cans of paint to add your own.
- Explore **Leake Street Arches**, which is home to the **Draughts Board Game Cafe** as well as places to eat and pop-up events and shops.
- Watch the bikers and skateboarders test out their tricks or hone your own skills at the **Southbank skatepark**.
- Look out for **street art** - constantly changing, you could find works by Stik, ROA and Bread Collective among others.
- Have a breather at the **Jubilee Gardens** playground.

NEED TO KNOW

It's easy to spend a whole day strolling the South Bank and stopping at various attractions, especially on a rainy day. Here are some tips on how long to allow for each.
- **Sea Life London:** around 2h
- **London Eye:** 60-90mins
- **Shrek's adventure:** 60-90 mins
- **London Dungeon:** 60-90 mins
- **Tate Modern:** 1-2h

36 | LONDONWITHKIDS.COM

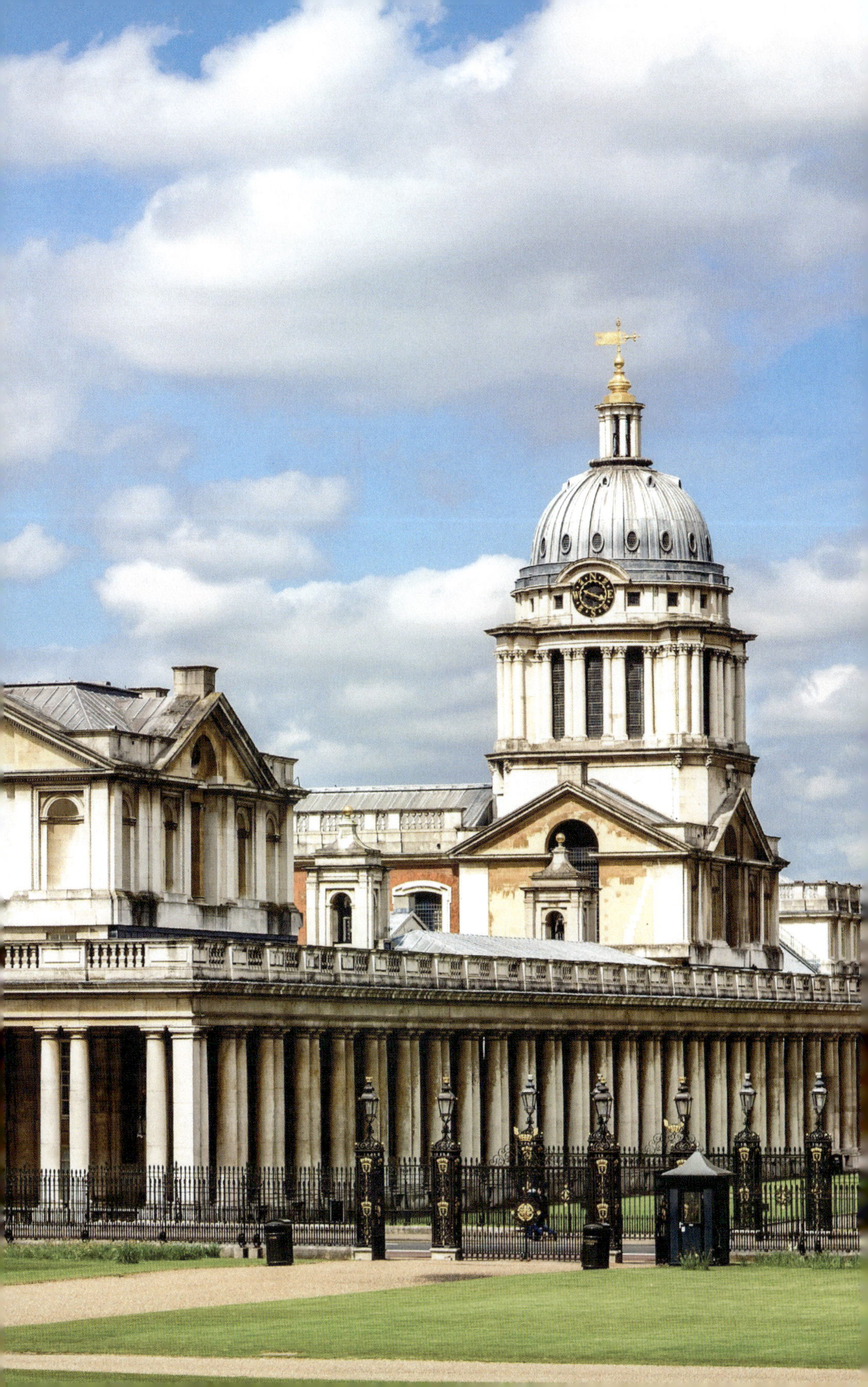

Day 6: Greenwich

MORNING

Greenwich is a bit of a journey from central London but it's well worth setting aside a day to spend here. And the best way to arrive is by boat to Greenwich pier, disembarking in the shadow of the **Cutty Sark**.

Start your day with a visit to the historic tea clipper, the fastest ship of her time. As well as children's trails, you can wander through the ship peeking inside cabins and exploring various interactive displays, before heading down to see the copper hull. Kids aged 10+ can try the **Rig Climb**, climbing up the rigging as sailors once did.

If the weather's good, **Greenwich Park** stretches for 183 acres with a play area, herd of deer, small lake and a viewpoint near the **Royal Observatory**. Save some time to explore **Greenwich Market** where you can grab food and shop for clothes, collectibles and souvenirs.

AFTERNOON

Visit another of Greenwich's Royal Museums this afternoon - you could head to the **Royal Observatory**, which contains London's only Planetarium. Older kids can also enjoy hearing the stories of the clocks that changed the world and tales of calculating the meridian.

The free **National Maritime Museum** traces Britain's maritime history, with a collection including maps, model ships and Admiral Nelson's coat. Explore the Great Map, learn about polar exploration and enjoy family activities during school holidays. Under-7s can also enjoy playing in the Ahoy gallery (prebooking advised, small fee at weekends).

Greenwich

The **Queen's House** completes the set - home to royalty for over 500 years, it now houses an art collection.

THE BIRTHPLACE OF TIME

Home to the **Prime Meridian**, Greenwich is the location used to calculate GMT and to measure every place on earth by its angle east or west from this point.

It runs across the **Royal Observatory Courtyard**, but you can also head to the viewpoint by the side of the building and go through the black gate by the big Shepherd clock to step over it for free.

ENJOY THE VIEWS

Find some rather different views at the North Greenwich peninsula:
- Take the **IFS Cloud cable car** to the Docklands, rising 90m up for a five-minute journey over the river.
- Get your heart racing by climbing 52m up onto the top of the **O2 Arena**. Kids must be 8+ and 1.2m tall to try Up at the O2.

Want more?
- Marvel at the Painted Hall in the Royal Naval College, Britain's Sistine Chapel.
- Visit the London Museum Docklands.
- Ice skate on the Queen's House rink (winter only).

Day 7: Camden

MORNING

Thanks to its markets and musical links, Camden has a justified reputation for being one of the coolest places in London. It's a great place to go with teens.

Start by exploring **Camden Markets**, a series of markets that make up most of the neighbourhood. The most prominent are **Camden Lock Market**, Stables Market, Buck Street Market, Inverness Street Market, and **Hawley Wharf**.

You can spend hours exploring the various stalls. When you need a break, **Camden Lock's West Yard Food Market** has street food vendors selling everything from Japanese curries to Vietnamese pho.

For dessert, head to **Hans & Gretel**, an ice cream shop covered floor to ceiling in candy canes, lollipops, cupcakes and colourful sweets.

AFTERNOON

If you're visiting with younger kids then you don't want to miss a visit to the **ZSL London Zoo**.

Right on the edge of the Borough of Camden, in Regent's Park, London Zoo is only a 20-minute walk from Camden Town.

The world's oldest scientific zoo, **London Zoo** is still one of the city's biggest attractions more than 170 years after it opened.

Camden

Once home to the bear that inspired Winnie the Pooh, the only living quagga ever photographed and one of the world's most famous giant pandas, there's almost as much history as animals.

London Zoo run family workshops during school holidays and you can even stay overnight at the Zoo, within roaring distance of the Asiatic lions (ages 5 and up).

GET ARTY

Camden is one of London's biggest **street art** hubs and has hundreds of amazing murals by some of the world's best street artists – including the one-and-only Banksy.

The best way to discover the stories behind the colourful murals is on a **Camden Street Art Tour** (suitable for all ages).

TAKE A RIVER RIDE

Camden is a great place to get out on the water with different options for cruising along Regent's Canal.
- The guided **Jenny Wren canal boat tour** lasts 90 minutes.
- **Jason's Trip Canal Waterbus** runs 45-minute trips on board a vintage narrowboat
- **The Music Boat** is a traditional Cambridge Punt accompanied by a musician.

Want more?
- Listen to music at The Roundhouse
- Play Plonk Crazy Golf
- Visit Babylon Park, an indoor amusement park

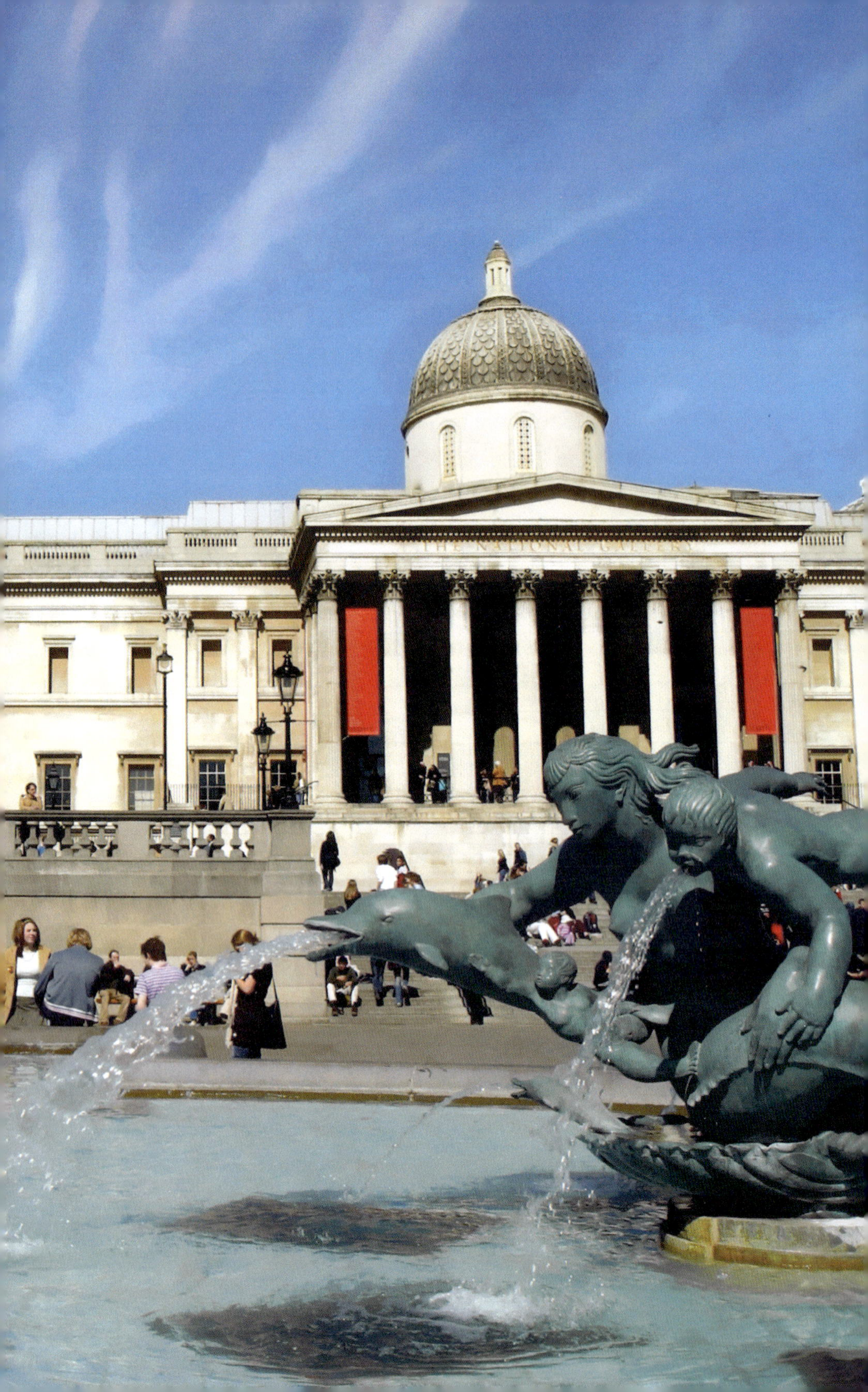
THE NATIONAL GALLERY

LONDON
THEMED ITINERARIES

Themed Itineraries: Welcome to Londinium

Almost 2,000 years have passed since the Romans established Londinium on the banks of the River Thames but centuries on, you can still spot Roman sites in London among the modern city.

THE OLD CITY WALLS

The **two-mile wall** stretching around Londinium was one of the biggest construction projects carried out in **Roman Britain**. One of the easiest sections to spot is near **Tower Hill tube station** - dating from 200AD, with a statue of the emperor Trajan in front.

THE MITHRAEUM

Hidden for centuries until it was rediscovered in 1954 in the basement of Bloomberg's European HQ, the **Roman temple of Mithras** was founded in the 3rd century. With interactive displays, the reconstructed temple is free to enter, but must be prebooked. The address is 12 Walbrook.

GUILDHALL YARD AMPHITHEATRE

Rediscovered in 1988, the remains of Londinium's amphitheatre is hidden away under **Guildhall Yard**. Trace the black line around the courtyard to see the original outline then head into the gallery where a surviving section showcases the entertainment that Londinium's citizens once enjoyed.

SOUTHWARK CATHEDRAL

The Romans' famous road network started on the south bank of the Thames, leading from Londinium to the south coast. **Southwark Cathedral** is home to a section - just after you enter the cathedral.

Welcome to Londinium

BILLINGSGATE ROMAN BATHS

The Romans famously loved their baths, and you can still visit one surviving set at **Billingsgate Roman House and Baths** at 101 Lower Thames Street. They're tucked away in the basement of an office block, with limited opening hours.

BRITISH MUSEUM

The **British Museum** collections trace 1,000 years of Rome's history, including a room on Roman Britain, with information on everything from the food eaten to the sports they watched.

FOLLOW IN ROMAN FOOTSTEPS

As well as ruins and remains of ancient sites, you can still walk in the footsteps of the Romans.

- **St Magnus the Martyr Church** - you'll find a timber from a Roman wharf at the entrance.
- **Fish Street Hill** - the heart of Londinium, one of Roman London's earliest streets.
- **Walk along the Thames** - Roman artefacts are still being unearthed from the river. They also built the first London Bridge, which crossed from St Magnus the Martyr church to Hay's Wharf (and today's Hay's Galleria) on the south bank.

Ave visitors! Put MMXXVI in your diary - that's 2026 if you prefer - when the **London Museum** - and its fantastic Roman collection - is due to reopen at its new site in Smithfield.

WELCOME TO CARNABY STREET

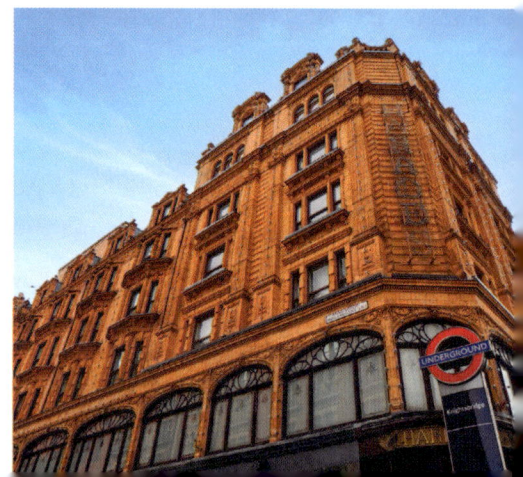

Themed Itineraries: Fashion Forward

London is one of the most influential fashion capitals in the world and where some of the most famous designers studied. Discover the best shops and sights fit for a fashionista

BEST FOOT FORWARD

Of London's 40,000 shops there are some that you simply can't miss. The designer department store **Liberty of London** opened in 1875, built from the timbers of two ships. It's famous for its fabrics department and unique 'Liberty prints'.

Selfridges is an emporium of fashion, homewares, make-up, kids' goods and much more spread over nine stylish floors.

Designer department stores **Harvey Nichols** and **Harrods** are located in Knightsbridge. Don't miss Harrods' famed Food Hall and Chocolate Hall.

On Piccadilly is **Fortnum & Mason**. Founded in 1707, it's famous for its luxury food hampers, tea and biscuits.

BEHIND THE SCENES

Don't miss the permanent Fashion collection at the **V&A Museum** in South Kensington. Spanning five centuries, the collection is the largest in the world, with rare gowns and post-war couture.

Founded by designer Zandra Rhodes the **Fashion and Textile Museum** is the only museum in the UK dedicated to showcasing contemporary fashion and textile design.

Fashion Forward

THE BEST SHOPPING STREETS

Shop 'till you drop along these popular streets:
- **Oxford Street** - the city's most famous shopping street and the busiest shopping street in Europe.
- **Regent Street** - a mixture of high street and high end shops.
- **Bond Street** - luxury designer stores.
- **Carnaby Street** - boutiques, concept stores, independent shops plus restaurants and bars.
- **The King's Road** - pivotal in the city's punk movement, today this road has some of the best shopping in town.
- **Savile Row** - famous for its bespoke men's tailoring outfitters.

THE BEST MARKETS

For vintage treasures and independent labels hit London's markets.
- **Portobello Green Market** - Portobello Road has antiques and collectibles, the Market is where you'll find vintage fashion (Fri-Sun).
- **Brick Lane Vintage Market** - vintage clothes from every decade starting in the 1920s (Sunday is the best day).
- **Old Spitalfields Market** - vintage gems and independent designers can be found in this market that's been going since the 13th century. (open daily).
- **Dover Street Market** - multi-storey clothes store great for urban streetwear brands (open daily).

Tea Time — The fashion-forward **Prêt-à-Portea** at The Berkeley hotel is the perfect afternoon tea for fashionistas with carefully crafted couture cakes celebrating famous designers..

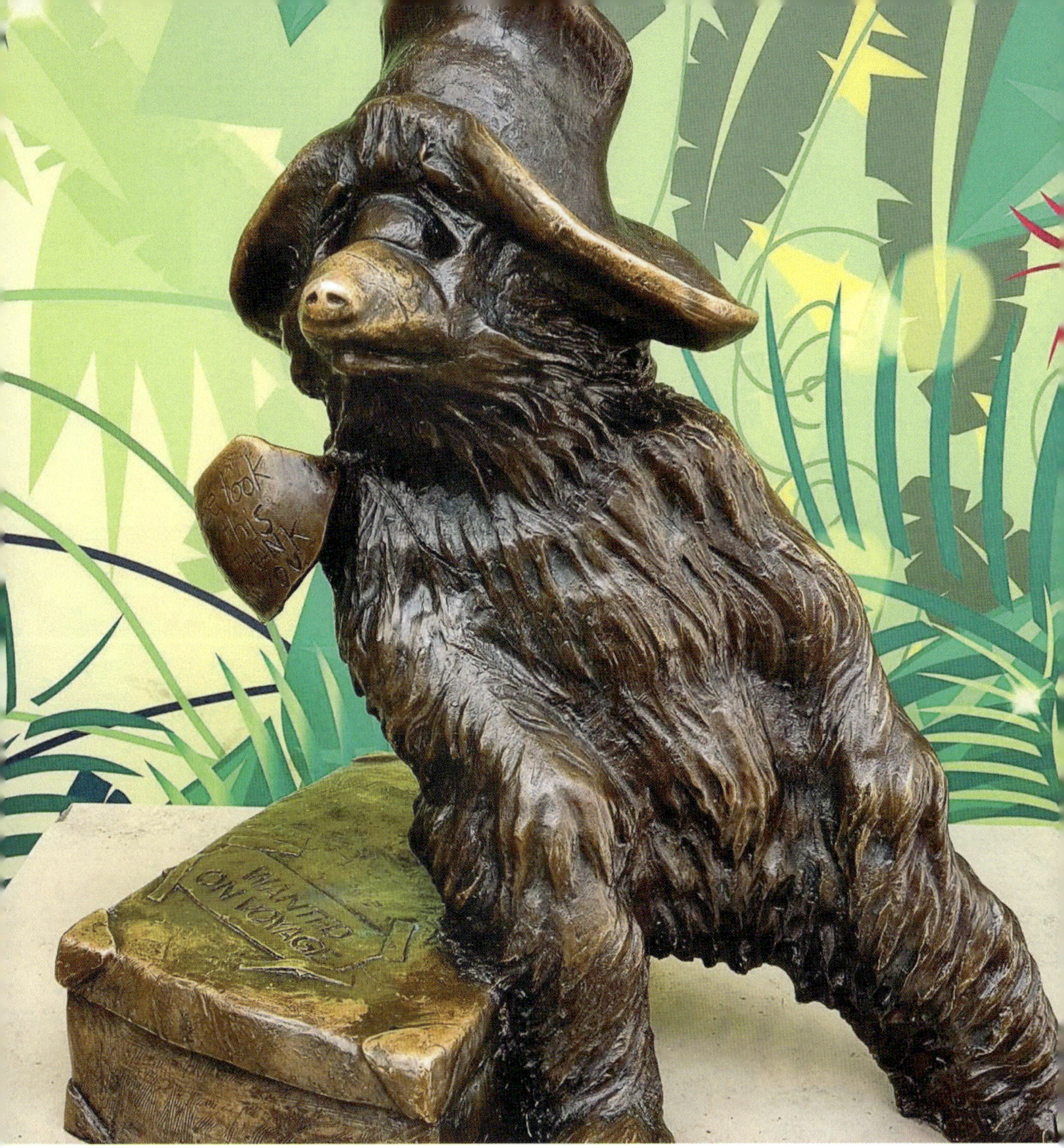
WANTED
ON VOYAG

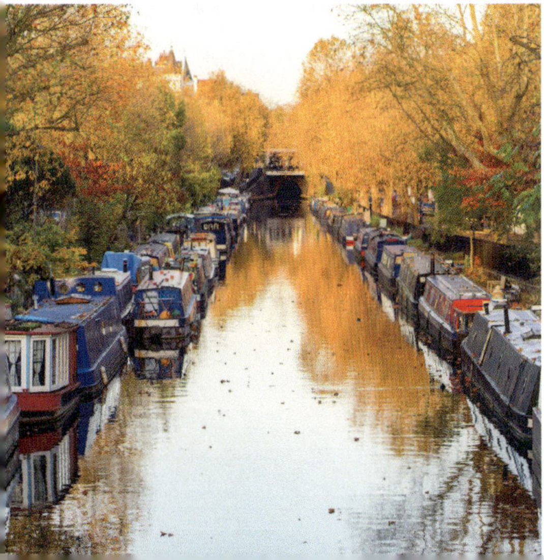

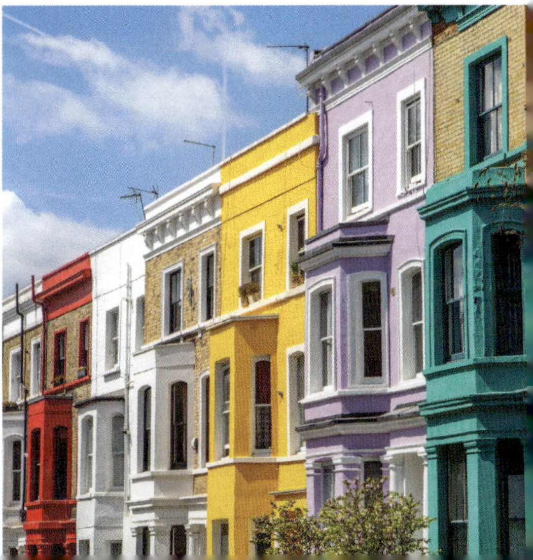

Themed Itineraries: Paddington Bear

Pack your marmalade sandwiches (duffel coats optional), because you don't need to travel to Darkest Peru to find Paddington Bear. Here's where to look in London.

SPOT THE STATUES

Start at **Paddington Station**, where the lovable bear first received his name - head to Platform 1 where you can spot a lifesize bronze statue.

Then take the station exit to the **Grand Union Canal**; heading north-west towards the Regent's Canal, you'll find the blue flock **Bearing Up** statue under the bridge, or turn the opposite way towards Paddington Basin to discover **Brick Bear** near Merchant Square.

A third statue, **Paddingtonscape**, spends its summers in **Norfolk Square Gardens** nearby, and its winters in the Hilton London Paddington.

Then stroll to **Paddington Green** where Paddington is commemorated along with his creator Michael Bond in St Mary's Churchyard.

In central London you'll find him relaxing with a sandwich in **Leicester Square** and the **Young V&A Museum** has a Paddington bear toy from 1980.

TEA FIT FOR A BEAR

The **Paddington Afternoon Tea Bus Tour** takes you past a string of London landmarks as you tuck into tea - including, of course, a great marmalade sandwich. There's guided commentary aboard the double-decker Routemaster bus, including Paddington's own tips.

Please Look After This Bear!

FOLLOW IN PADDINGTON'S PAWPRINTS

Want to make your own bear-themed walking tour? Here are some of the key book and filming locations along with Paddington station itself.

- **Portobello Road** - where the little bear would go for elevenses at Mr Gruber's antiques shop.
- **Selfridges department store** - Michael Bond bought the original bear which inspired the stories from the Oxford Street store (which has a distinct resemblance to the fictional Barkridges department store of the books).
- **Little Venice** - the canal towpath was the scene of a highspeed chase in the second film.
- **The Natural History Museum** - the South Kensington Museum was the site of the first movie's dramatic climax.

TAKE A PADDINGTON WALKING TOUR

Join a **guided tour** from Paddington station to some of the filming locations from the movies as well as places mentioned in over 15 books, including Little Venice and Portobello Road. Run by **Brit Movie Tours**.

Bear with me!

There's no point trying to find **32 Windsor Gardens** – author Michael Bond combined his address with his parents' to create the Brown family home and the only real-life Windsor Gardens in London doesn't have a number 32. The closest you'll get is **Chalcot Crescent** in Primrose Hill, used as the Browns' home in the movies.

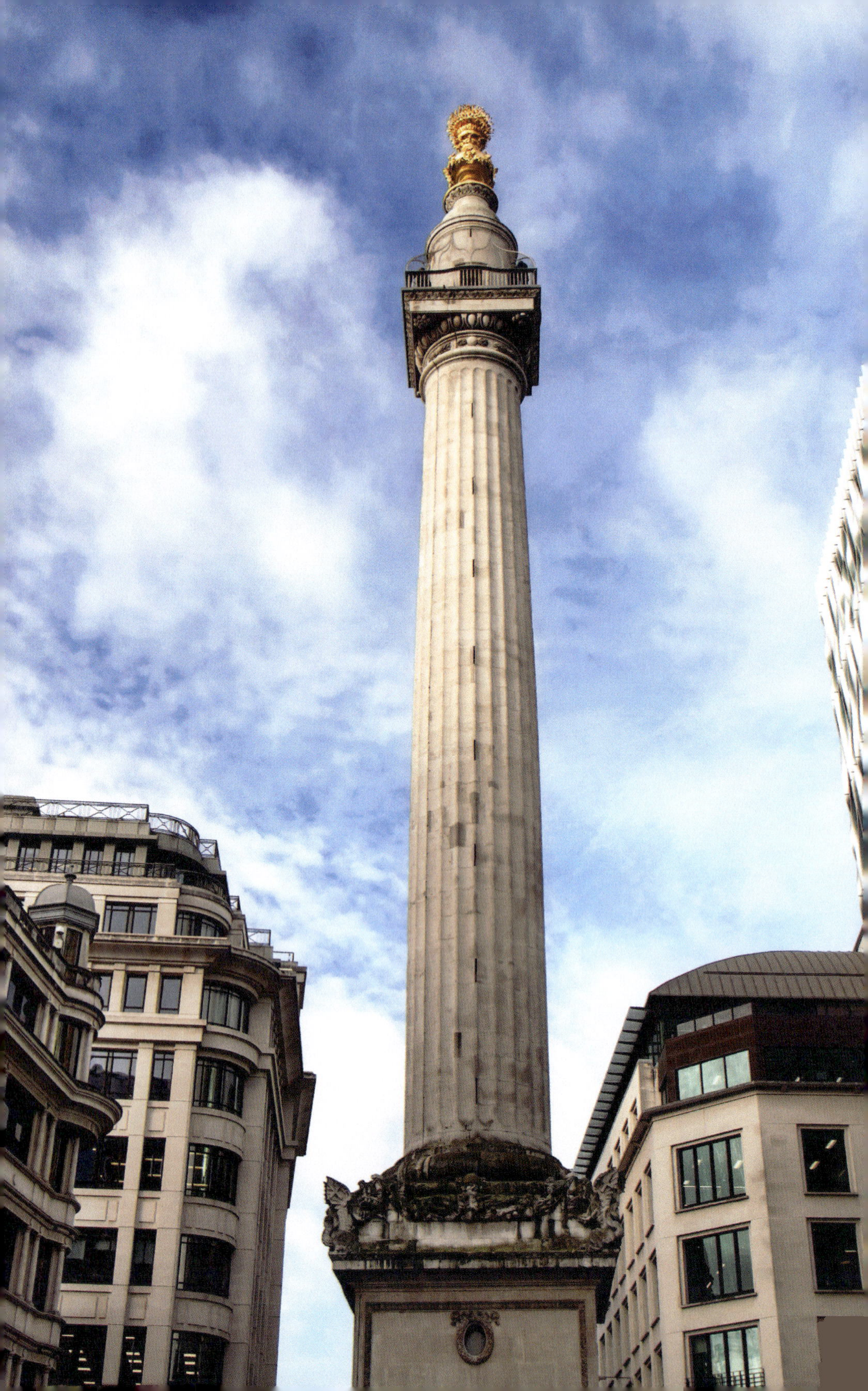

Themed Itineraries: London's Burning

In 1666, a chance spark from a baker's oven led to a four-day conflagration which burned down 13,000 homes and left around 100,000 of London's inhabitants homeless. Responsible for transforming the face of the medieval city, you can still visit some of the key locations.

PUDDING LANE

Where else should you start but **Pudding Lane**, home to the bakery where the fire began. Conspiracy theories have abounded over the years but the first spark came from an oven belonging to Thomas Farynor or Farriner, a baker who lived on the street.

A plaque marks the spot, while nearby blocks are marked with the lines of the children's song London's Burning – 'London's burning, London's burning. Fetch the engines, fetch the engines. Fire fire! Fire fire! Pour on water, pour on water'.

ST PAUL'S CATHEDRAL

The original medieval **St Paul's** was in a bad state of repair before the fire, but no-one could agree whether to restore it or demolish it and start again… until the fire made the decision for everyone.

Today it's hard to imagine London's skyline without **Christopher Wren's famous dome**, one of the highest in the world. You can visit except on Sundays or when it's closed for special services, climbing to the galleries and seeing tombs of famous Britons in the crypt, including Wren himself and Samuel Johnson whose diary records his experience of the fire.

London's Burning

THE MONUMENT

Just steps away from Pudding Lane, at the junction of Monument Street and Fish Street Hill, is the most famous spot commemorating the fire. Known simply as **the Monument** it was designed by Sir Christopher Wren and finished in 1677.

Standing 202 feet high, it's 202 feet from the spot where the fire started on Pudding Lane - if you laid it down, it would reach right to the bakery. You can climb the 311 steps to the gallery for views across the city.

SITES THAT SURVIVED THE FIRE

While the Great Fire razed much of London to the ground, a handful of buildings have survived.

- **Staple Inn** - one of only four original Tudor timber-framed buildings left in the City of London, the mid-16th century Staple Inn is a glimpse of what the streets might have looked like before. It sits near the Chancery Lane tube exit on High Holborn.
- **41 Cloth Fair** - the oldest house in the City of London, built between 1597 and 1614. Both it, and the 16th century St Bartholomew's Gatehouse were saved by the nearby priory's thick walls.
- **All Hallows by the Tower** - the oldest church in the City of London, Samuel Pepys climbed its tower to watch the fire spreading.

Look Out! Find the fire mark in **Goodwin's Court**, an old alleyway off St Martin's Lane. The small gold and red crest on the wall showed the house was protected in case of fire, one of many to be seen in the days before fire brigades.

Themed Itineraries: Get Sporty

London is home to every sport possible from indoor cricket and crazy golf to ice skating, skateboarding and more (plus stadium tours for footie fans). Here's our pick of the best sporting activities in London.

LORD'S CRICKET GROUND

Cricketing fans should head to **Lord's Cricket Ground** for a tour of the Grade II listed Victorian Pavilion, home to an unrivalled collection of cricket-related art and memorabilia.

INDOOR CRICKET AT SIXES

Sixes is an indoor immersive cricket experience under special UV lights, that allows wannabe Sachin Tendulkars the chance to swing for six.

TOCA SOCIAL AT THE O2

Football fans will enjoy **TOCA Social**, an interactive football experience. Book a private box for 60 or 90 minutes, choose a level that works for you (beginner, intermediate or advanced) and get ready to score.

JUNKYARD GOLF

Play a round of crazy mini-golf on one of four **Junkyard Golf** courses created from, well, junk and named Pablo, Bozo, Dirk or Gary

LEE VALLEY VELO PARK

For fun on two wheels, head to the **Lee Valley Velo Park** where teens can tackle the track in the iconic velodrome, race on the road circuit, attempt the mountain bike trails or jump on the BMX track.

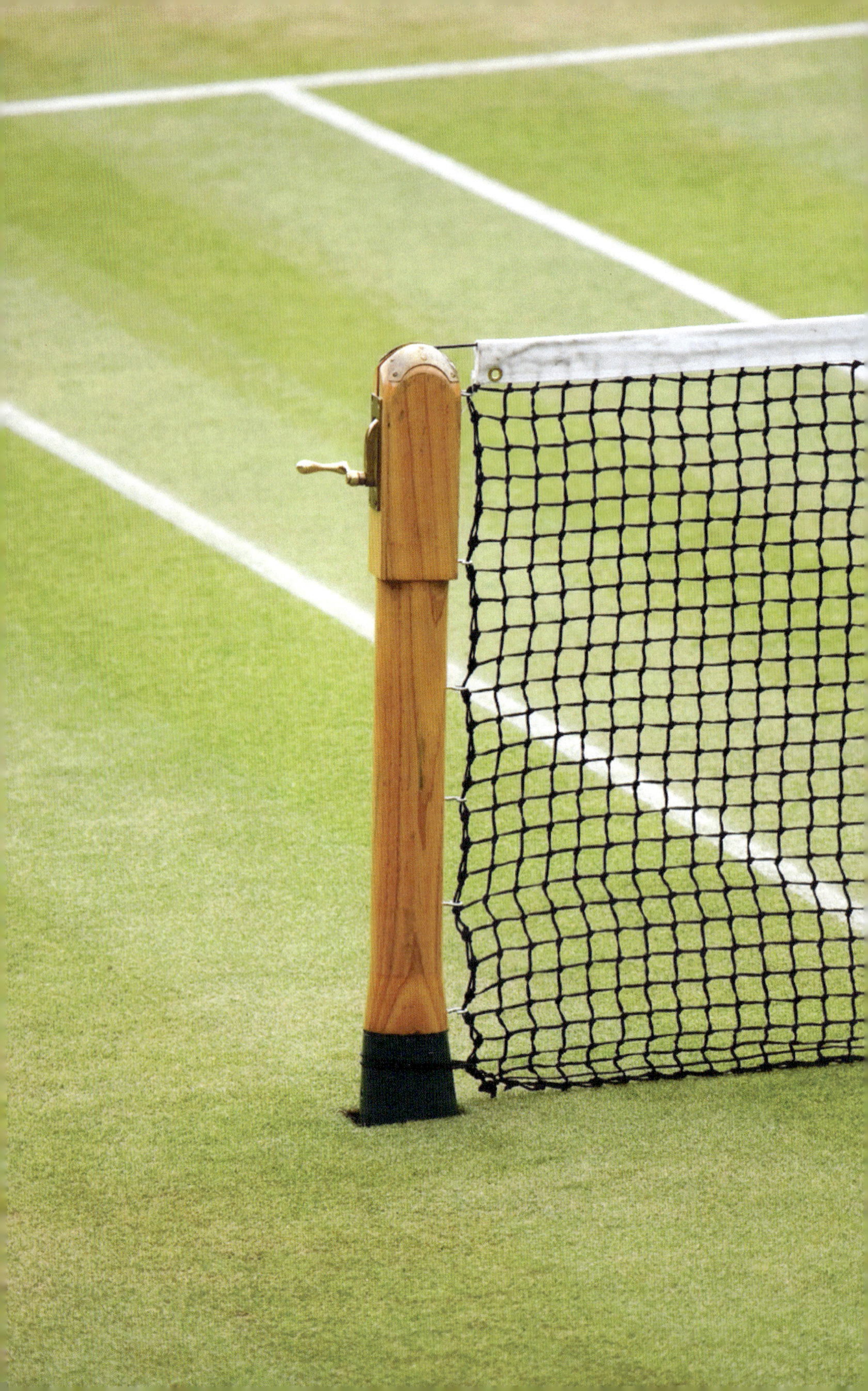

Get Sporty

KICKABOUT

Football fans can enjoy tours at the new **Tottenham Hotspur** stadium, the **Arsenal Emirates Stadium** and **Fulham FC**. There's also the award-winning tour of the **Chelsea** grounds and 90-minute tours are offered at **Wembley Stadium**, UK's largest sports and music venue.

TOP WATERSPORTS

When the sun's out, keep cool in the water:

- **Stand Up Paddleboarding** - Paddington Basin and Kew Bridge both offer SUP session for families.
- **Wakeboarding** - **WakeUp Docklands** in Royal Victoria Beach is London's only cable wakeboard park conveniently within the central transport network (min age 10).
- **White Water Rafting** - **The Lee Valley White Water Centre** is the closest venue near London for white water rafting and was the venue for the canoe slalom events in the London 2012 Olympics.
- **Kayaking & Canoeing** - **Moo Canoes** offer kayak and canoe hire on London's waterways from Easter until the end of October.
- **Swimming** - There are plenty of places to make a splash including **outdoor lidos** in Park Road Crouch End, Tooting Bec or at London Fields. Outdoor swimming opportunities include **Hampstead Ponds** (age 8+) and, for serious swimmers, the **West Reservoir** (age 14+).
- **Windsurfing** - Try **Queen Mary Reservoir** or **Canary Wharf**.

LONDONWITHKIDS.COM | 57

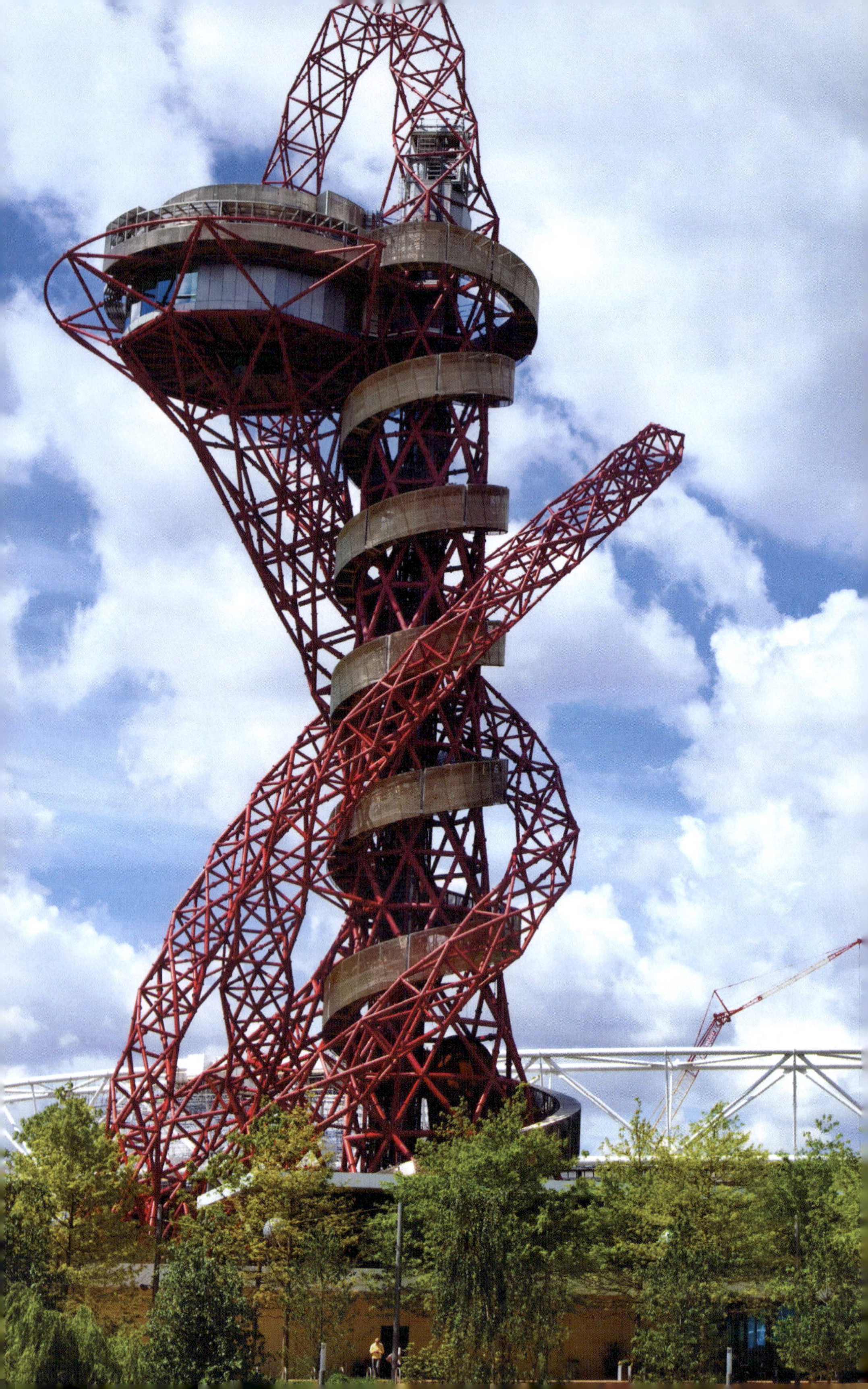

Themed Itineraries: Thrills and Spills

Think that London is nothing but sights and museums? Think again! The capital is packed with daredevil activities guaranteed to thrill.

ARCELORMITTAL ORBIT SLIDE

Not only is the **ArcelorMittal Orbit** the UK's tallest sculpture at 114.5-metres high, it's also home to the world's longest tunnel slide. Located in Queen Elizabeth Park the epic slide has 12 twists and turns including the 'bettfeder', a tight corkscrew that translates as the 'bedspring'.

CLIMB THE O2 ARENA

Clip in and walk over the roof of the **O2 Arena** in London's Greenwich Pensinula. This multi-purpose arena hosts concerts, sports and theatre but the best way to see it is from up high. Choose from a daytime, sunset or twilight climb (age 8+).

GO APE

The biggest of the three **Go Ape** London locations is **Alexandra Palace**, which combines thrills with great city views. Here you'll find the Treetop Adventure, Treetop Adventure Plus and Treetop Challenge – the latter includes the Plummet, a 12m free fall toward the forest floor. The other two locations are at **Battersea Park** and at **Cockfosters**.

TEAM SPORT

Get your motor running and head off on a go kart track for some guaranteed fun. **Team Sport** has five indoor karting tracks (age 8+).

Thrills and Spills

GO ABSEILING

Are you brave enough to try the UK's highest freefall abseil from the country's tallest sculpture? Run by **Wire & Sky**, the abseil takes place from the upper viewing platform of the ArcelorMittal Orbit at 262ft where professional instructors are on hand to guide you.

THAMES ROCKETS

Witness some of London's best sights while you zip along the Thames River in a bright red speedboat. **Thames Rockets'** tours include the Ultimate London Adventure, a 50-minute ride at 30 knots that takes in sights from Big Ben to Tower Bridge and the 80-minute Thames Barrier Explorers Voyage that runs from the London Eye to the Thames Barrier.

DARE SKYWALK

Walk across the roof of Tottenham Hotspur's new stadium, the largest club stadium in London, on a thrilling 90-minute journey. The highlight of the **Dare Skywalk** is the glass walkway positioned 46.8 metres above the pitch, just above the penalty spot.

ROCK CLIMBING

Located in North London is **The Castle**, the UK's largest climbing Centre. Housed within a Victorian former pumping station the centre has 450 routes and 90 roped lines. They also offer bouldering options.

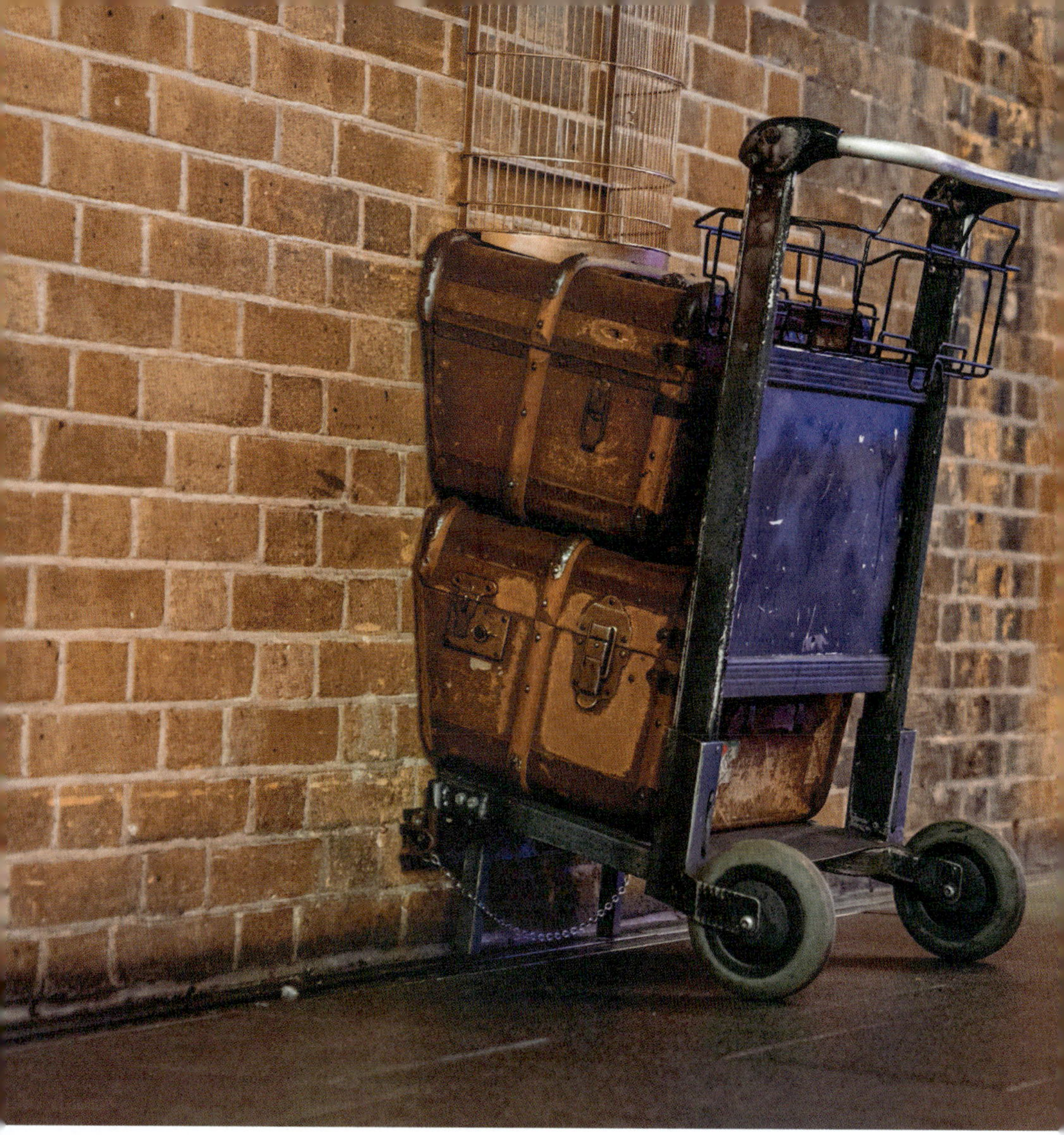

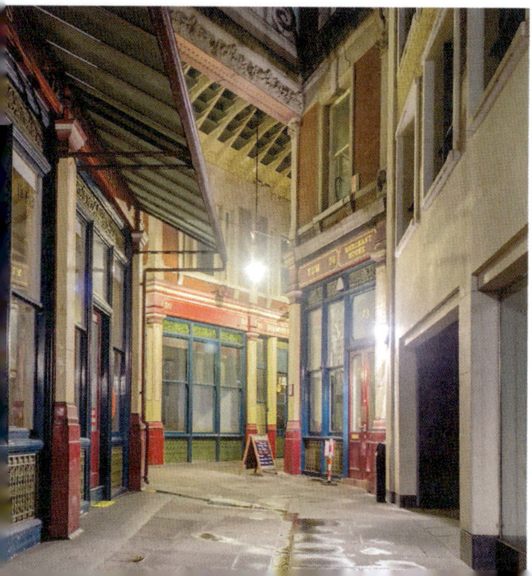

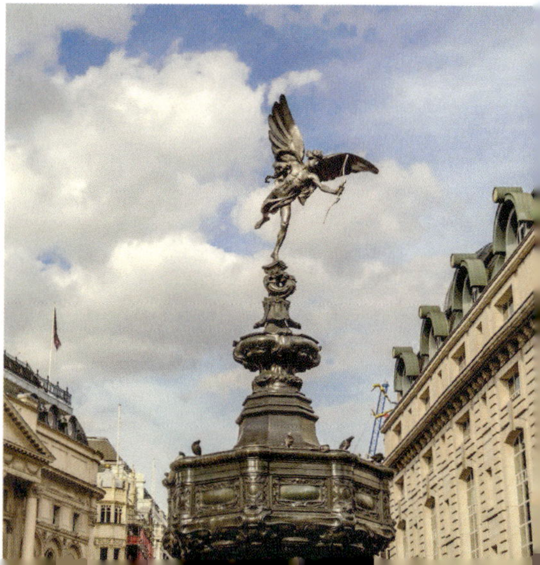

Themed Itineraries: Wizarding Fun

If you love the wizarding world, you can find countless Harry Potter filming locations in London, plus places which are mentioned in the books and even historic spots thought to have inspired JK Rowling.

WARNER BROS STUDIO TOUR

Unmissable for Harry Potter fans, the **Warner Bros Studio Tour** is only 20 minutes by train from Euston followed by a shuttle bus transfer.

From the Great Hall and Forbidden Forest to the Hogwarts Express, Gringotts, Diagon Alley, and more, there are genuine props, behind-the-scenes secrets and a chance to meet magical creatures from the movies.

Plus you can try your hand at **riding a broomstick,** casting spells and even drink some butterbeer. Book well in advance, especially for peak season and special events.

VISIT PLATFORM 9 3/4

Start your journey through Harry Potter's London at **Kings Cross station**. We can't promise you'll find the Hogwarts Express, but you can pose with a luggage trolley at **Platform 9 ¾**. Platforms 4 and 5 were actually used for filming, if you want to see the genuine location.

HOUSE OF MINA LIMA

Graphic design duo Miraphora Mina and Eduardo Lima – aka **MinaLima** – were the brains behind everything from the Marauder's Map to Bertie Bott's Every Flavour Beans. Their gallery and shop is on Wardour St.

Wizarding Fun: Top Filming Locations

- **St Pancras Renaissance Hotel** - next door to Kings Cross, this is the view when Harry and Ron flew off in the Weasleys' Ford Anglia.

- **Leadenhall Market** - in the first movies, the entrance to Diagon Alley is in this Victorian covered market. Find the curved door by the optician in Bull's Head Passage.

- **The Market Porter Pub** - by Borough Market, this appears in the third movie. The building next door doubled as the Leaky Cauldron.

- **Claremont Square** - the unusually-shaped Islington Square doubled as Grimmauld Place.

- **The Millennium Bridge** - stretching between the Tate Modern and St Paul's Cathedral, it's attacked by Death Eaters in the sixth movie.

- **Cecil Court and Goodwin's Court** - near Charing Cross Road and St Martin's Lane, they're said to have inspired Diagon Alley and Knockturn Alley. Watkins Books even sells 'dragon's blood' as well as the kind of books you might find in Flourish & Blotts.

- **Piccadilly Circus** - Harry, Hermione and Ron apparate here to escape the Death Eaters in the Deathly Hallows Part One, so if you're ticking all the Harry Potter London locations off, you should at least stroll through.

Wands out! Try wand-making at the **Wizard Exploratorium** on Greek St. in Soho, where you can also enjoy a **Wizard Afternoon Tea** or **Potions Experience** for more magical fun.

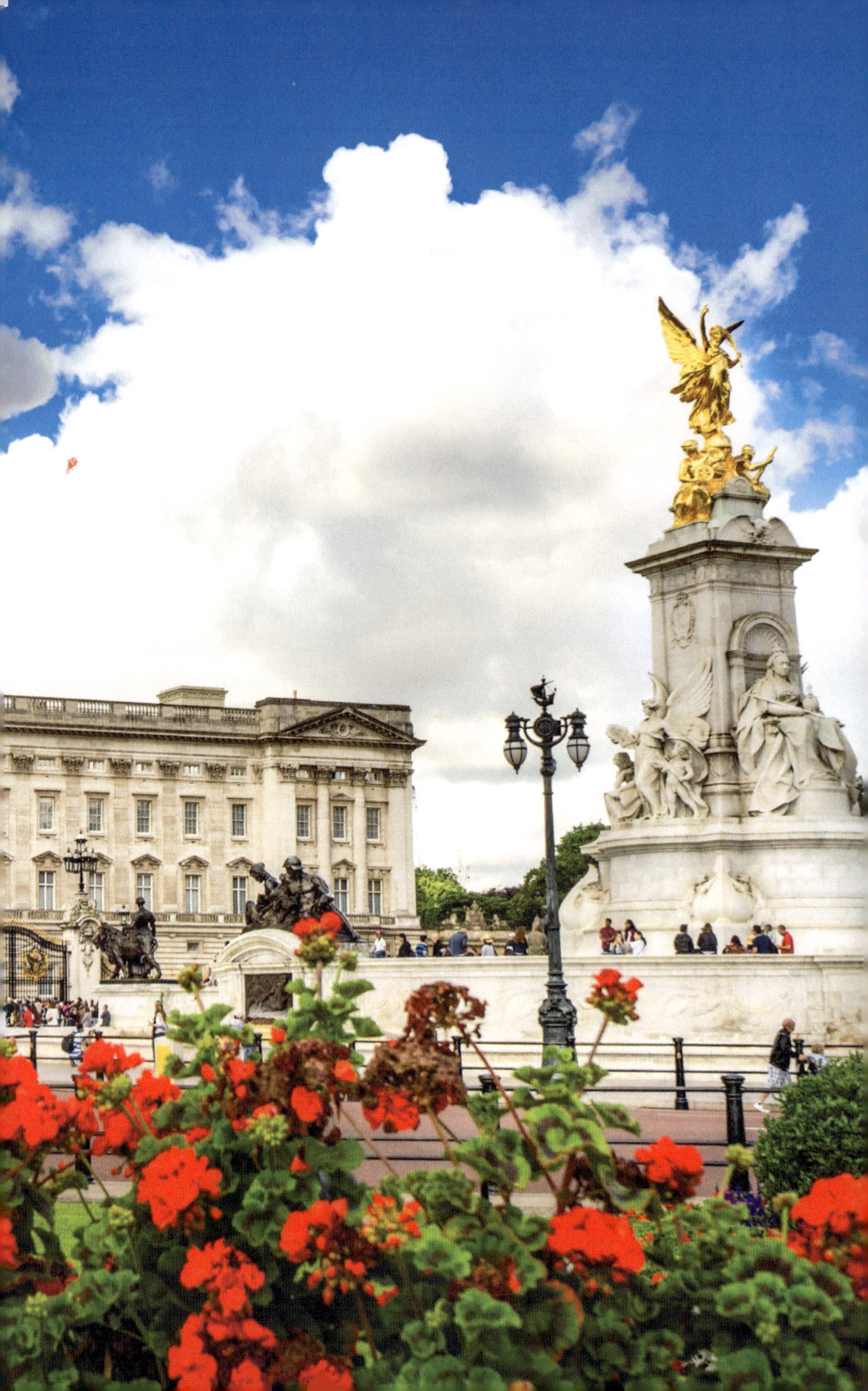

BEYOND THE SIGHTS
LONDON LIKE A LONDONER

10 Unmissable Things in London

If only have time to do 10 things in London, make sure that these are on the list.

1 TOWER OF LONDON

One of London's most famous sights, the **Tower of London** boasts almost 1,000 years of history and is home to the Crown Jewels. Plan to spend half a day here.

2 CHANGING OF THE GUARDS

The **Changing of the Guards** ceremony takes place outside Buckingham Palace, and marks the moment when the soldiers on duty exchange places with the New Guard. It's a ceremony that dates from the reign of Henry VII.

3 LONDON TRANSPORT MUSEUM

The brilliant **London Transport Museum** charts the history of London's transport system through hands-on fun.

4 NATURAL HISTORY MUSEUM

London's **Natural History Museum** is one of the best London attractions for families. The Dinosaur Gallery is home to an enormous animatronic Tyrannosaurus Rex. There's an earthquake simulator, Hope the blue whale and the most intact Stegosaurus fossil ever found.

5 SCIENCE MUSEUM

The **Science Museum** is filled with fascinating scientific discoveries from across the ages. Most of the museum is free to enter but it's worth paying the entrance fee for Wonderlab, a hands-on magical world of science.

6 BUCKINGHAM PALACE

One of London's most popular and iconic sights, **Buckingham Palace** has served as the official London residence of the UK's sovereigns since 1837. Tours of the State Rooms take place in summer months.

7 TOWER BRIDGE

Not to be confused with London Bridge just down the river, beautiful **Tower Bridge** was built between 1886 and 1894. Walk across it or pay to go inside and explore. At certain times of day the bridge raises to allow river traffic through.

8 TRAFALGAR SQUARE

See the stone lions, eye up Nelson's column, snap a photo by the fountains and enjoy the many free events that take place throughout the year.

9 SOUTH BANK

The River Thames runs through the heart of London and one of the best ways to appreciate it is with a walk along the **South Bank**. Home to the Southbank Centre, National Theatre and BFI Film theatre as well as restaurants and pubs. You can even search for treasure on a mudlarking tour.

10 LONDON EYE

Get a bird's-eye view from the **London Eye**, the revolving ferris wheel on the bank of the river. Other options for great city views include the **Sky Garden**, London's highest public garden, **Horizon 22** and **The Shard**, London's tallest building.

10 Hidden Gems in London

Once you've ticked off the main sights, enjoy these hidden London gems...

1 THE POSTAL MUSEUM

Covering the history of the Royal Mail, the **Postal Museum** is definitely not just for stamp collectors. Ride the Mail Rail train, play in the Sorted! play area (age 8 and under), discover the postal system's quirky past and more.

2 THE GOLDEN HINDE

Journey back to Tudor times on board the **Golden Hinde**, near London Bridge, a replica of the ship which Francis Drake sailed around the world.

3 LEAKE STREET GRAFFITI TUNNEL

Unleash your inner Banksy in the **Leake Street Graffiti Tunnel** near Waterloo Station. Grab a can of paint and get creative or join a workshop.

4 THE OLD OPERATING THEATRE MUSEUM

Step inside a 19th century **operating theatre**, the oldest surviving surgical theatre in Europe. Housed in the attic of an early 18th century church, part of the old St Thomas's hospital, it's a great option for teens and wannabe surgeons.

5 DISCOVER CHILDREN'S STORY CENTRE

Get lost in stories at **Discover: Children's Story Centre** in Stratford, aimed at kids under 12. The multi-sensory play space features two floors of magical Story Worlds and Story Garden, plus timed activities along with special exhibitions.

6 PUPPET THEATRE BARGE

The UK's only **floating puppet theatre** has been delighting audiences with puppet shows for over 40 years. Moored in Little Venice the 50-seat theatre has regular children's performances.

7 CHELSEA PHYSIC GARDEN

The fascinating mix of plants at the **Chelsea Physic Garden** makes it a lovely place to visit. There are often children's trails and special workshops, as well as the glasshouses to explore.

8 GO BOAT

Head out on a self-drive adventure at the helm of one of the electric boats from **GoBoat**. There's a choice of four London locations: Paddington, Canary Wharf, Kingston and Thames Ditton

9 CHARLES DICKENS MUSEUM

Charles Dickens' former home in Doughty Street has been converted into a museum dedicated to his life and work. The site where he wrote some of his early books, including Oliver Twist, is furnished as it would have been in 1837. Regular family events take place in the holidays.

10 WORD ON THE WATER

Browsing books has never been more fun than at this **bookstore on a canal barge**, moored near Granary Square, Kings Cross. Find kids' books among the titles stacked on indoor and outdoor shelves at Word on the Water.

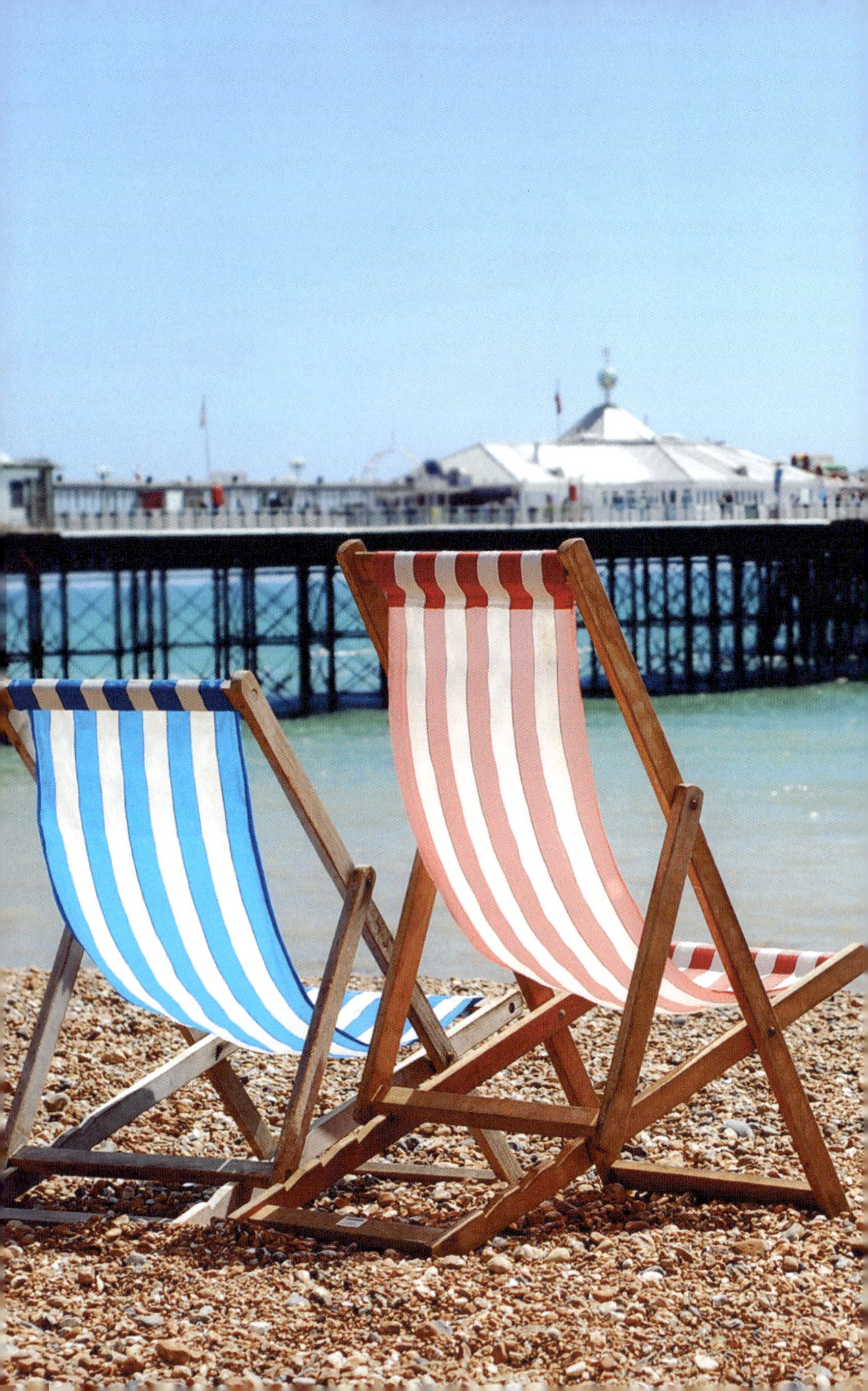

LONDON
DAY TRIPS

LONDONWITHKIDS.COM | 71

Best Day Trips from London

As much as we love London, sometimes it's good to escape the city. The following are some of our favourite day trips.

HAMPTON COURT

A short train journey from Waterloo, this **Tudor Palace** easily fills a day trip on its own - as well as exploring the historic apartments, there are gardens and grounds, the famous maze and a great children's playground to discover.

Travel details: London Waterloo - Hampton. Around 40 minutes.

STONEHENGE

There is nowhere in the world quite like **Stonehenge** – this amazing prehistoric creation still has the power to fascinate at any age. While it's tricky to reach if you don't have a car, the standing stones and museum are worth the effort. Easy to combine with a stop in Salisbury too.

Travel details: London Waterloo - Salisbury. Around 90 minutes plus 30 minute bus or a taxi ride.

BATH

Pretty **Bath** is ideal whether your kids are fascinated by Roman places, love the writing of Jane Austen or the Regency elegance of the architecture. Don't miss the **Roman Baths** themselves, and save time to try a famous Bath bun before browsing the shops on Pulteney Bridge.

Travel details: London Paddington - Bath Spa. Around 70-90 minutes.

WINDSOR

Home to the world's **oldest working palace**, the royal family still spends weekends at **Windsor Castle**, where you can watch the Changing of the Guard, eye up a spectacular doll's house belonging to Queen Mary, see royal tombs including that of Henry VIII in St George's chapel, as well as exploring the state rooms.

Travel details: London Waterloo - Windsor & Eton Riverside. Around 55 minutes. London Paddington - Windsor & Eton Central. Around 30-40 minutes via Slough.

OXFORD

There's something for everyone in **Oxford**, from the historic college buildings to the botanic gardens, pretty riverside and museums galore. The **Oxford Story Museum** is ideal for kids who love reading, as you'll find links to Harry Potter, Narnia and His Dark Materials here. Or punt along the river to see Oxford from the water.

Travel details: London Paddington - Oxford. Around 45 minutes.

THE COTSWOLDS

With their honey-coloured stone, pretty villages and rolling green hills, the **Cotswolds** are the picture-postcard image of England. Scattered across several counties, mostly Gloucestershire and Oxfordshire, the villages and attractions of the Cotswolds are best explored by car.

Travel details: London Paddington - Moreton-in-Marsh. Around 90 minutes.

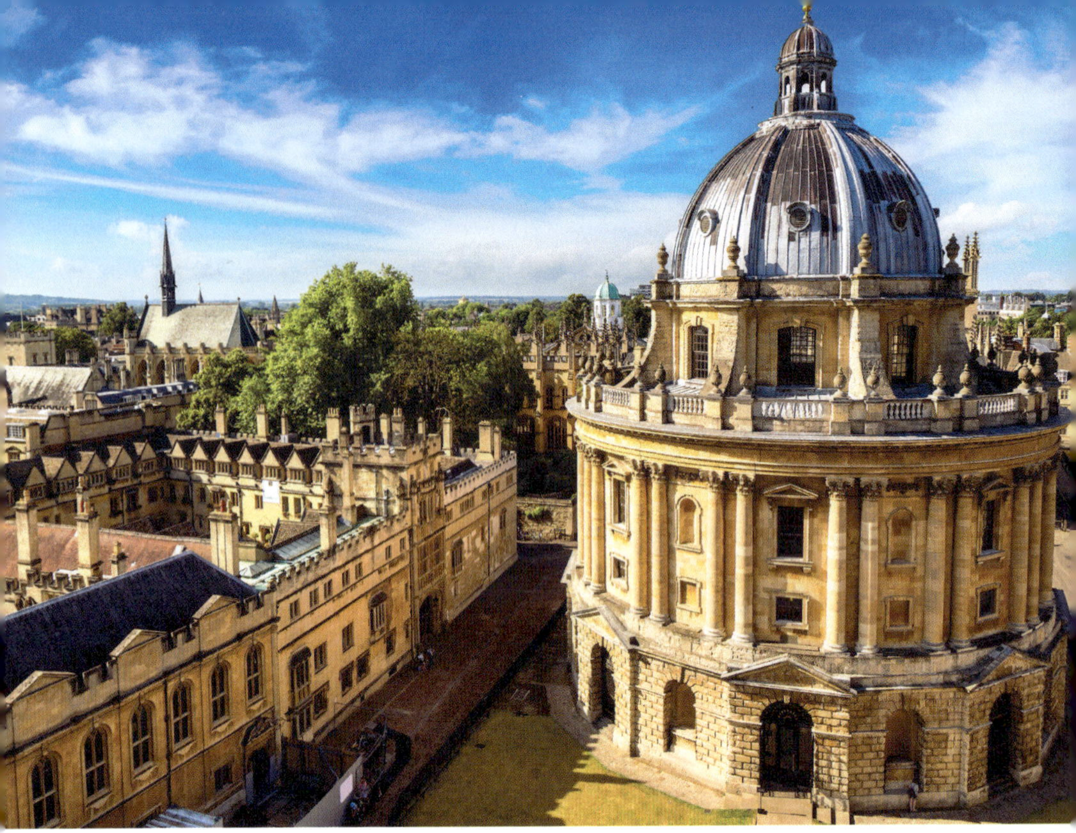

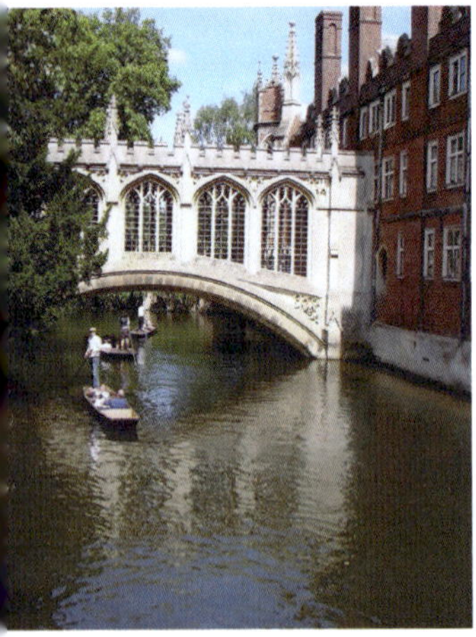

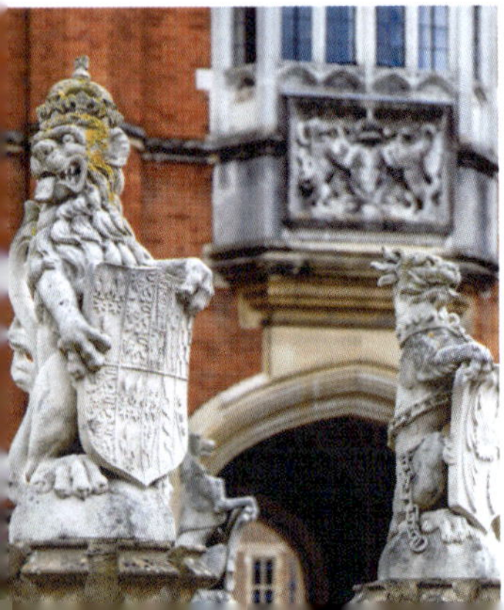

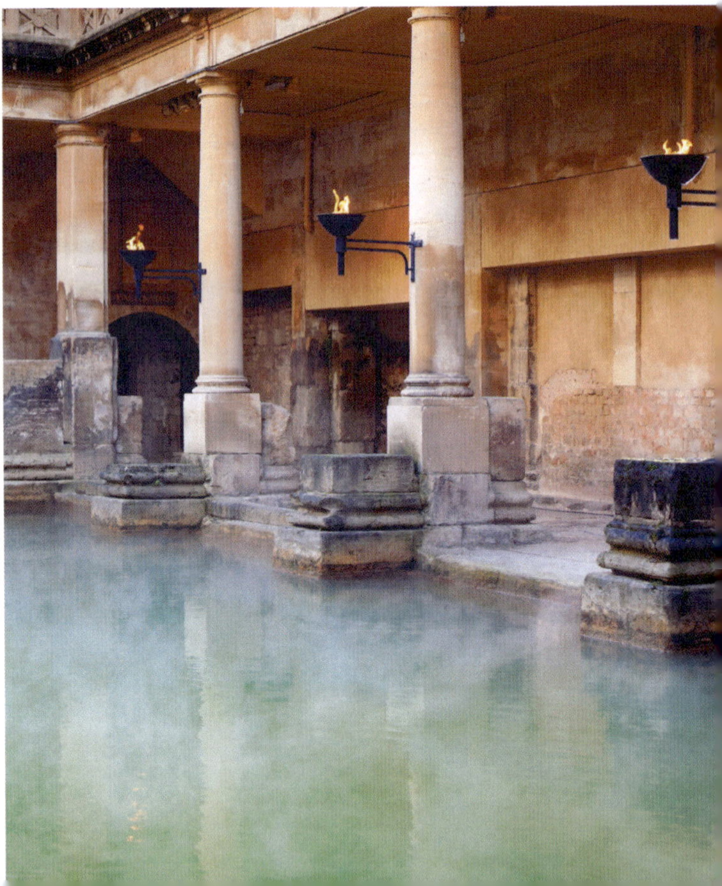

CAMBRIDGE

The second of England's most prestigious university cities, **Cambridge** has great museums and art galleries, including child-friendly activities, more colleges to explore, botanic gardens and its own stretch of river to discover by boat.

Travel details: London Kings Cross/Liverpool Street - Cambridge. From around 50 minutes.

BRIGHTON

One of the closest stretches of coast to London, **Brighton** is one of the easiest day trips if you fancy hitting the beach. Check out the attractions on the pier, the quirky shops of the Lanes, George IV's opulent Royal Pavilion, and the world's oldest aquarium while you're there too.

Travel details: London Victoria - Brighton. Around one hour. Trains also run from London Bridge and Blackfriars, taking around 70 minutes.

THEME PARKS

There are also several fun theme parks within easy distance of London including:
- Become a Master Builder at **Legoland Windsor** (travel to Windsor as before, and take a shuttle bus from the station).
- Go wild at **Chessington World of Adventures** (travel from London Waterloo to Chessington South + bus/short walk).
- Scream on the rollercoasters at **Thorpe Park** (travel from London Waterloo to Staines + 950 Express bus).

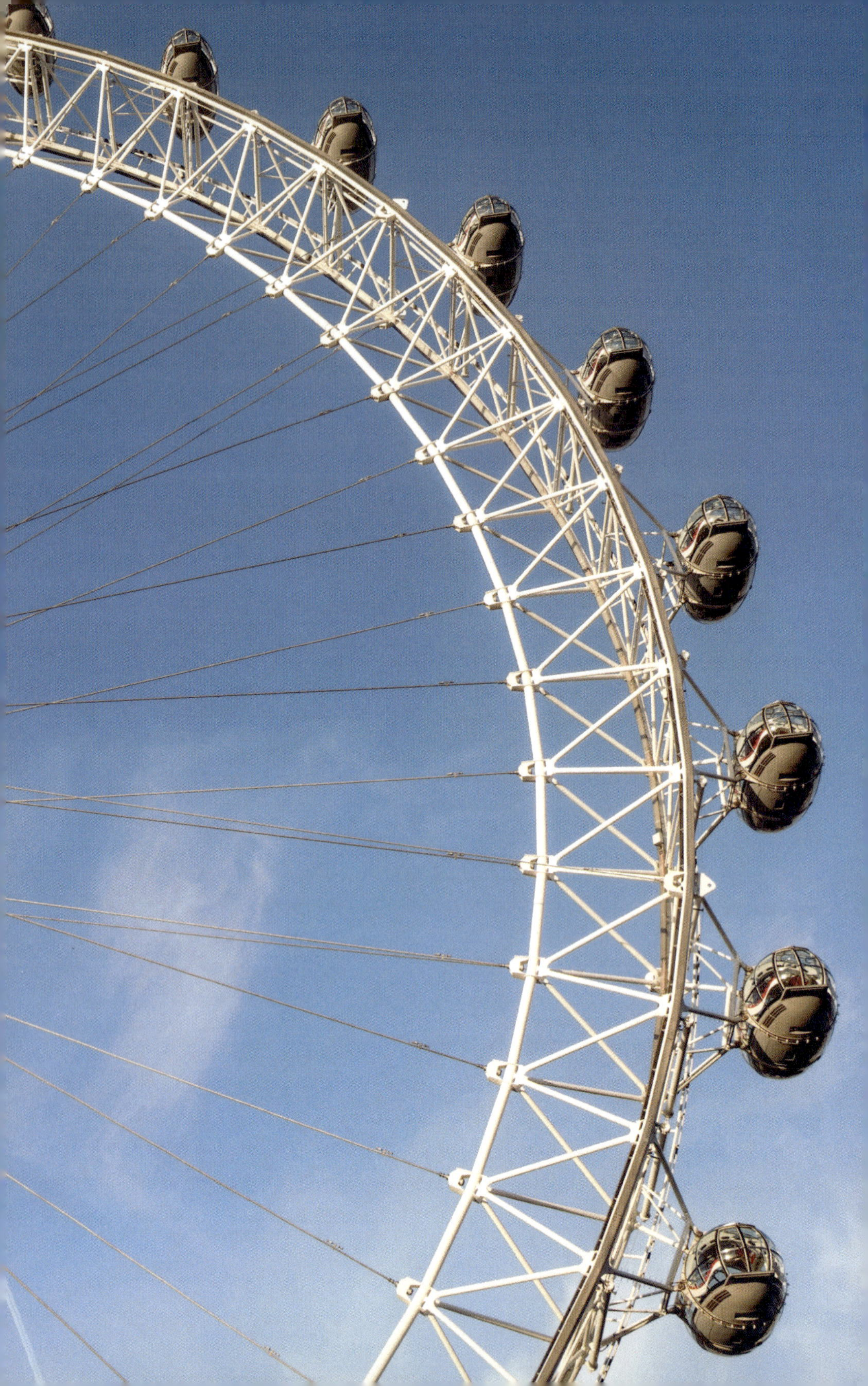

LONDON
OUTDOORS

London's Best Views

Get a bird's-eye view of London's incredible skyline from one of these top spots..

1 THE LONDON EYE

The **London Eye** is a giant ferris wheel standing 135 metres tall on the South Bank of the River Thames. Visitors revolve slowly around in glass pods enjoying panoramic views of the city.

2 ONE NEW CHANGE

Head to the **Roof Terrace of One New Change** shopping centre for spectacular free views over London's skyline.

3 THE SHARD

Measuring 310m, **The Shard** is London's tallest building and the 95-storey skyscraper is home to the UK's highest viewing gallery, The View from The Shard.

4 THE SKY GARDEN

For free views head to the **Sky Garden** at the top of the Walkie Talkie building. This is London's highest public garden with 360-degree views over the city. Prebooking tickets is recommended.

5 IFS CLOUD CABLE CAR

Soar above the London skyline in the **IFS Cloud cable car.** The 10-minute journey links the Greenwich Peninsula to the Royal Docks.

6 TOWER BRIDGE

The high-level walkway at **Tower Bridge**, London's most famous bridge, is a popular spot for seeing highlights including views of The Shard and St Paul's Cathedral.

7 THE ROOF OF THE O2 ARENA

You can see great views of London from the **O2 Arena** – when you walk over the rooftop! This fun experience is a great way to see the London skyline.

8 THE DARE SKYWALK

The 90-minute Dare Skywalk adventure takes you to the top of **Tottenham Hotspur's stadium**. Look down and see the penalty spot directly below you, look around and enjoy a unique panorama of the north London skyline.

9 LONDON ABSEIL WIRE & SKY

Witness spectacular views of London with an adrenaline rush while dangling from the **ArcelorMittal Orbit**, 80 metres above the ground. This is the UK's highest freefall abseil.

10 HORIZON 22

Enjoy London's highest free viewing platform and see the city from 254 metres up.

11 THE HERON TOWER

Enjoy breakfast, lunch or dinner with a view in the **Heron Tower**. Located on floors 38 and 39 is **SushiSamba** and Europe's highest outdoor dining terrace. On the 40th floor, with floor to ceiling windows, is the **Duck and Waffle** open 24hrs.

12 KING HENRY'S MOUND

Located in **Richmond Park**, this prehistoric burial chamber from the Bronze Age is the highest point in the park. It was once used as a viewpoint for hunting by King Henry VIII.

LONDONWITHKIDS.COM | 79

London's Great Outdoors

Get out and about and enjoy some of London's best parks, gardens, rivers, waterways and more.

ST JAMES'S PARK

Head to **St James's Park** for great views across the water towards Buckingham Palace and to meet the pelicans who live here: the latest in a long line of the birds since the 17th century.

KENSINGTON GARDENS

One of London's royal parks, **Kensington Gardens** is also home to the excellent Diana Memorial Playground, set around a huge pirate ship.

HYDE PARK

Splash around in the Diana Memorial Fountain in **Hyde Park**, soak up the views in a deckchair by the Serpentine lake or book a ride and explore the leafy park on horseback.

REGENT'S PARK

Time your visit right and you can see more than 12,000 roses in Queen Mary's Gardens in **Regent's Park.** The park is also home to London Zoo, four playgrounds and rowing boats to hire on the lake.

GREENWICH PARK

The oldest royal park, **Greenwich Park** has its very own herd of deer living in the south-eastern corner. Go boating on the lake and enjoy fantastic views of the city by the Royal Observatory.

PADDINGTON RECREATION GROUND

Spread over 27 acres in central London, **Paddington Recreation Ground** is home to sports facilities plus an incredible playground for young kids with a dedicated space for teens.

QUEEN ELIZABETH OLYMPIC PARK

Built for the 2012 London Olympics, the **Queen Elizabeth Olympic Park** is now a brilliant play space with the Tumbling Playground, Waterworks Fountains and the 114.5m-tall ArcelorMittal Orbit slide.

HAMPSTEAD HEATH

Escape Central London for a trip to **Hampstead Heath** - the 800 acres of woodland inspired C.S. Lewis to write The Chronicles of Narnia.

THE SOUTH BANK

Discover London's history with a walk along **the South Bank** and the Thames – the river has always been at the heart of the capital. Spot major landmarks including the Houses of Parliament, St Paul's and the Tower of London along the way.

CRYSTAL PALACE PARK

Located in south London, **Crystal Palace Park** is home to 30 life-size model dinosaurs that were the talk of the town when they were unveiled in 1854. Restored in 2002 they are now Grade I listed.

HOLLAND PARK

Home to an adventure playground for kids aged up to 14, **Holland Park** also has the Kyoto Garden, with koi carp, waterfalls and peacocks.

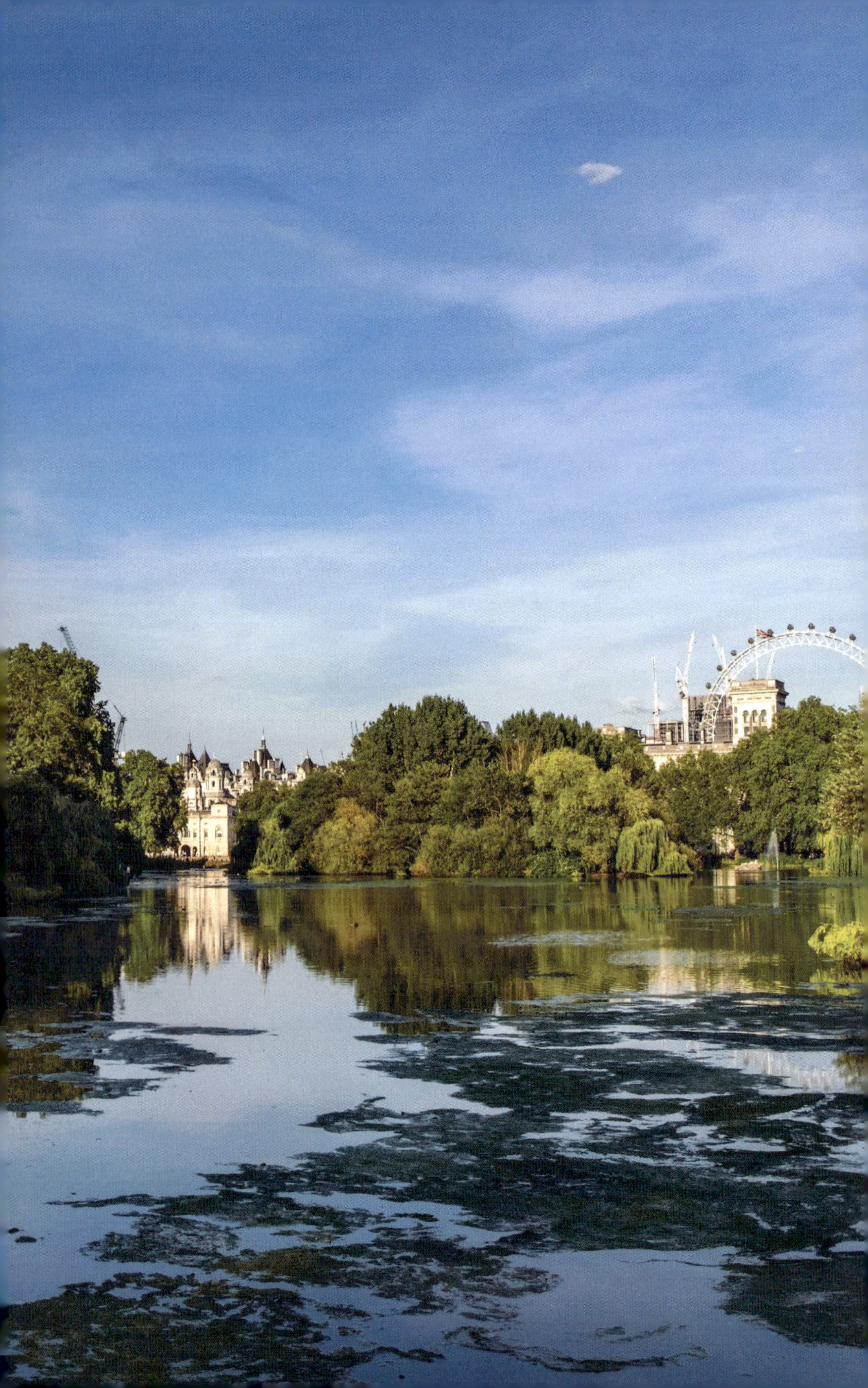

LONDON RESTAURANT FAVOURITES

Best Places to Eat

There are *lots* of great places to eat in London with kids, the following are just some of our favourites.

HARD ROCK CAFE

For fun, fast food head to one of the two **Hard Rock Cafes** and enjoy great burgers, a good kids' menu and lots of rock memorabilia.

WAHACA

The colourful chain of Mexican restaurants delivers good value tacos, tostadas and a good kids' menu.

DISHOOM

Head to **Dishoom** for their house black daal, delicious curries and their sausage naan roll. Excellent for breakfast, lunch and dinner, plus they have a kids' menu.

PIZZA PILGRIMS

There are branches of **Pizza Pilgrims** around town. Come for their excellent pizzas, tasty toppings and good kids' menu.

INAMO

The food at **Inamo** is very good (a mixture of Japanese, Chinese and Thai dishes) but kids will love the interactive tables most.

UZUMAKI

Japanese anime fans should make a beeline for **Uzumaki**, a colourful ramen and sushi shop inspired by the character Naruto.

HOLBORN DINING ROOM

For a grown-up meal where younger diners are welcome, head to **Holborn Dining Room** which serves up plenty of British classics including excellent pies.

BREAD STREET KITCHEN

Run by Gordon Ramsay, the **Bread Street Kitchen** serves British staples including Shepherd's Pie and Beef Wellington with a kids' menu.

GORING DINING ROOM

Celebrating a special occasion? Book a table at the **Goring Dining Room**, a Michelin-starred restaurant and Royal Family favourite that warmly welcomes kids with a dedicated menu.

POPPIE'S FISH & CHIPS

Enjoy excellent fresh fish and chips (with a side of jellied eels if you like) at **Poppie's Fish & Chips**, retro-fitted family-run restaurants in Camden, Soho and Spitalfields.

APRICITY

One of the most unique dining experiences for kids can be found at **Apricity** run by chef and owner Chantelle Nicholson. This Green Michelin-starred restaurant is the only London venue to offer a children's tasting menu.

BOROUGH MARKET

Borough Market is London's oldest food market, home to dozens of delicious food stalls selling everything from paella and sandwiches to freshly shucked oysters and empanadas.

MAXWELL'S BAR & GRILL

Maxwell's is an American-style family-run diner that serves family-friendly favourites such as burgers, mac'n'cheese and BBQ ribs. The most popular items on the menu are the elaborate Freakshakes.

MILDREDS

For tasty plant-based plates head to **Mildreds**, a popular vegan restaurant with six sites across town. Favourites include curries and quinoa bowls alongside BBQ pok buns, and grilled artichoke Caesar.

Best Places for Treats

What's travel without a treat or two? Indulge after all that walking and sightseeing with a few of these

CHIN CHIN LABS

Using huge vats of quick freezing liquid nitrogen to create the gourmet ice cream, it's a little like wandering into Willy Wonka's chocolate factory at **Chin Chin Labs**.

MILK TRAIN CAFE

This quirky ice-cream parlour in Covent Garden is home to the UK's first candy floss ice-cream cones - plus **Milk Train** has seasonal specials too.

BAKE

For the tasty Asian-inspired desserts try **Bake** in Chinatown, including fish-shaped Taiyaki pastries filled with custard, bean paste, or Nutella.

THE KNOT CHURROS

Cute and quirky, **The Knot Churros** cafe in South Kensington serves up delicious and indulgent Spanish churros with all the toppings.

BUBBLEWRAP

Bubblewrap first brought the Hong Kong street snack to London, teaming ice cream with crunchy waffle. Now in Old Spitalfields Market, Westfield Stratford and Chinatown.

HUMBLE CRUMBLE

Found in foodie hot spots of Borough Market and Old Spitalfields Market, **Humble Crumble** specialises in the traditional British dessert of crumble, topped with torched meringue.

MAXWELLS

Maxwell's Bar & Grill in Covent Garden is famous for its Freakshakes, piled high with cake, donuts, chocolate, cream & more toppings.

HANS & GRETEL

Based on the Brothers Grimm's tale, Camden Market's **Hans & Gretel** is a magical dessert cafe, covered from floor to ceiling in candy canes, lollipops & sweets galore.

MAITRE CHOUX

The first and only choux pastry specialist patisserie in the world, **Maître Choux** has locations in South Kensington, Kings Road and Soho. The mini chouquettes are great to share.

RUBY VIOLET

Small, independent ice cream parlour **Ruby Violet** in Kings Cross also has fabulous hot chocolate as well as its own cakes and bakes.

CUTTER AND SQUIDGE

Most famous for their biskies – a cross between a cake and a biscuit – you won't be short of sweet treats and bakes at **Soho's Cutter & Squidge.**

BREAD AHEAD

Fancy more than just eating delicious desserts? Take a look at **Bread Ahead**, which runs baking courses as well as selling its doughnuts and other baked goodies. Branches in Borough Market, Sloane Square and South Kensington.

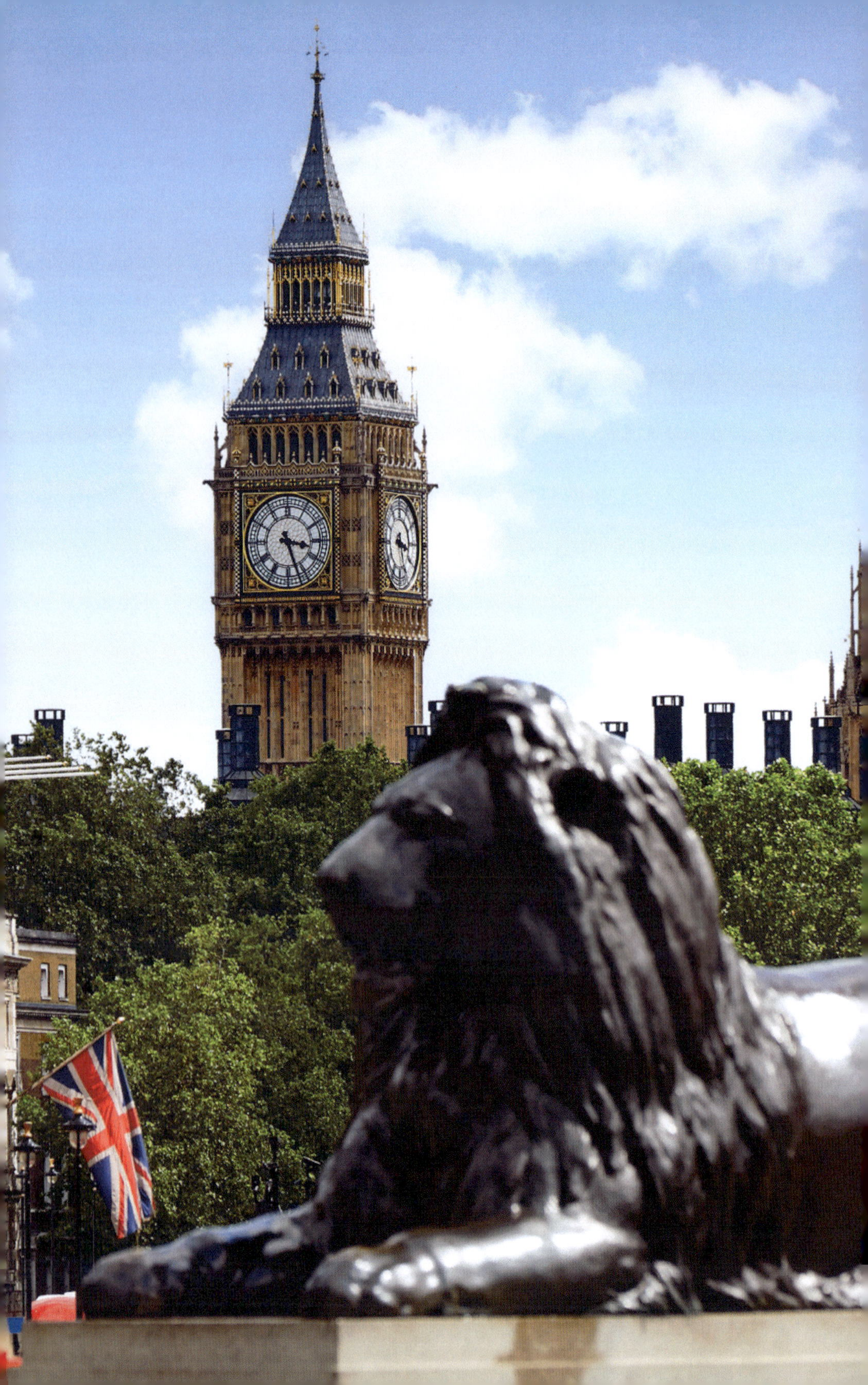

LONDON
WHERE TO STAY

London's Best Family Hotels

Choosing where to stay in London with kids can be one of the biggest dilemmas when planning a family holiday to London. Fortunately, there are lots of great family hotels in London from boutique boltholes and luxury five-star stays to budget-friendly hotels in fantastic locations.

Location

Where you stay depends a lot on who is travelling with you. If you're visiting with **toddlers**, for example, it's worth staying in a **central location** near the main sights and parks so you don't have to travel too far every day.

Teenagers on the other hand, will love neighbourhoods such as **Camden** and **Shoreditch**. These are a little cooler and a little busier than some of the central London neighbourhoods.

Budget

There are some incredible **family-friendly hotels in London** but they can be expensive. Some of the best come with dedicated kids' concierges, afternoon tea, design-led family rooms, **swimming pools**, and more.

There are also some **excellent value hotels**, such as the Premier Inn chain, that offer convenient locations, family rooms and wallet-friendly prices.

If you are staying for longer than four nights then you may want to consider renting an **AirBnB** or **serviced apartment**.

Availability

If your family vacation is planned for peak months such as October half-term, Christmas, Easter and summer then be aware that prices will be higher and availability lower. Make sure you book well in advance

Best Budget Hotels

Some of the best value hotels in London belong to the family-friendly Premier Inn chain. There are some 70 Premier Inn hotels in London, many of them just a short walk from some of the city's best sights including the London Eye, the Southbank, the Tate Modern, and the Tower of London.

PREMIER INN COUNTY HALL

Positioned in the Grade II listed County Hall building and within walking distance of the London Eye, its central location is hard to beat.

PREMIER INN LONDON SOUTHWARK BANKSIDE

This branch is located just a short walk from Southwark underground station and London Waterloo

PREMIER INN LONDON BANK

Close to Monument underground station, this branch is near to the Tower of London, St Paul's Cathedral and the Sky Garden.

PREMIER INN LONDON ST PANCRAS

Perfectly positioned for catching trains in and out of London, as well as the Eurostar to Paris.

TRAVELODGE LONDON CENTRAL MARYLEBONE

Another popular and reliable budget chain of hotels, their family rooms sleep up to four people and kids under 15 eat free.

YHA LONDON CENTRAL

This is a great budget option. It has private rooms with bunk beds and ensuite bathrooms as well as private rooms with shared bathrooms.

COMFORT INN VICTORIA

Housed within a renovated Georgian house this hotel offers no-frills family rooms that can sleep up to four people.

YOTEL LONDON SHOREDITCH

Wallet-friendly modern hotel with family rooms sleeping four. Rooms are on the smaller side.

Best Midrange Hotels

THE Z HOTEL COVENT GARDEN
If you're looking for a central address then this is an excellent choice. The rooms aren't large but they offer fantastic value in a great location. The Z Family rooms sleep 4 in a set of double bunk beds.

HOLIDAY INN CAMDEN LOCK
Offers family rooms with a kids stay and eat free programme. Kids under 18 stay free when sharing a family room and children under 12 also eat free from the kids' menu (when accompanied by at least one full paying adult).

DOUBLETREE BY HILTON LONDON KENSINGTON
Located in Shepherds Bush near the underground and Westfield London shopping mall, this hotel has interconnecting rooms for families and pretty views over the public garden..

LONDON MARRIOTT HOTEL REGENT'S PARK
This perfectly positioned hotel near Regent's Park has family rooms that sleep up to four people in two double beds.

LA GAFFE
Located in Hampstead, North London, this award-winning family-run guesthouse has been welcoming guests (including The Beatles!) since the 1960s. It has two family rooms, one with bunkbeds and the other a full-sized single bed. An additional roll away bed can be added to this room.

THE HILTON LONDON OLYMPIA
Located on Kensington High Street, this midrange hotel has family rooms and interconnecting rooms and children under 12 eat free.

Best Luxury Hotels

ST. ERMIN'S HOTEL

Once the meeting point for British spies, today this luxury family-friendly hotel is one of the best places to stay in London with kids. Its family rooms sleep five, there are gifts for kids and they do an excellent afternoon tea.

HOTEL CAFÉ ROYAL

This hotel has the Royal Nanny Seal of Approval owing to its partnership with Louenna Hood, trusted Norland Nanny to numerous royal families. Expect family-friendly rooms, custom children's menus, specially crafted trunks and more.

THE MARYLEBONE

This lovely luxury hotel has interconnecting rooms and suites for families plus gifts for children upon arrival, milk and cookies at bedtime, children's toiletries, board games, babysitting and more.

ATHENAEUM HOTEL & RESIDENCES

Located opposite Green Park, the hotel offers interconnecting rooms and private Residences with kitchenettes and bunk beds. Guests can borrow kites to fly in Green Park and bikes to cycle around Hyde Park.

RUBENS AT THE PALACE

Located on Buckingham Palace Road, kids can sleep in monarch-themed bedrooms, take part in a pastry class, enjoy a dedicated afternoon tea and more at this family-friendly hotel.

DUKES HOTEL

A short walk from Buckingham Palace, family amenities at Dukes include complimentary breakfast, Dukes Scavenger Hunt, personalised monogrammed bathrobes for the kids, a Dukesy the Dog to take home and a dedicated family concierge.

Best Hotels that sleep 5+

HILTON METROPOLE

Located not far from Edgware Road underground stations, and walking distance to Marble Arch, the hotel's biggest rooms will sleep five.

DOUBLETREE BY HILTON LONDON DOCKLANDS RIVERSIDE

Housed in a 17th century building, once home to London's last dry shipbuilding dock, there are some fantastic views out onto the river and several different room options for families of five.

ZEDWELL PICCADILLY

The Cocoon rooms at Zedwell Piccadilly don't just sleep five, there's room for six, eight and even 12, which is a real rarity in London – let alone so close to Piccadilly Circus. There are no windows or natural light though.

PARK PLAZA HOTELS

The Park Plaza hotels have some of the best locations in London, including properties at Victoria and on Westminster Bridge, with two-bedroom apartments suitable for a family of five or six.

CLARENDON HOTEL

A little further out of the centre, this hotel near Greenwich has a family suite with double and three single beds, and is great if you're travelling on a budget.

YHA YOUTH HOSTELS

With several locations around the city and private rooms sleeping five, these hostels are a great option for bigger families, with properties at Earl's Court and central London, not far from Oxford Circus.

Best Hotels with Pools

THE LANGHAM

One of the city's most luxurious hotels, set overlooking Regent Street, this London instition has its own 16m long pool, as well as family rooms and its own children's programme.

HOLIDAY INN LONDON KENSINGTON

One of the few hotels in London with a pool if you're travelling on a budget, this hotel is also perfectly located for the South Kensington museums, and walking distance from Kensington Gardens and Hyde Park. No family rooms but there are connecting rooms.

NYX HOTEL LONDON HOLBORN

A short walk from the British Museum and Covent Garden, this hotel is a great option for older kids and teens - as well as the 13m infinity edge pool, you can find retro arcade games in the lobby.

ONE ALDWYCH

This elegant hotel is located right in the heart of London, just off The Strand, and housed in an Edwardian building. As well as interconnecting rooms and suites, there's an 18m pool with underwater music and projections of sea creatures.

THE LANDMARK LONDON

Another of London's top luxury hotels, there are special children's activities as well as family rooms and family packages to book. The 15m chlorine-free heated pool is one of the big highlights for kids though - swimming cap essential.

THE DILLY

Set just off Piccadilly, this luxury hotel is home to one of the largest indoor swimming pools in central London, plus family rooms, children's activities and family-friendly afternoon tea.

LONDONWITHKIDS.COM

MIND THE GAP

LONDON RESOURCE GUIDE

Festivals & Events

There's always something going on in London - the following are some of the main events. If visiting during popular times such as Christmas and the summer holidays, make sure to book your accommodation well in advance.

JANUARY

Watch the lively London **New Year's Day Parade** march through central London on January 1 and then the colourful **Chinese New Year Parade** (Lunar New Year generally falls between Jan 21 and Feb 20).

FEBRUARY

Get dressed up for **London Fashion Week** and perfect your pancakes for **Shrove Tuesday**. Pancake flipping races take place in Greenwich and Borough Markets. **February Half Term** brings family fun.

MARCH

Watch the colourful **St Patrick's Day Parade** through central London, join events across the city marking **Ramadan**, and switch on at the **London Games Festival.**

APRIL

Watch the annual free staging of **The Passion of Jesus** in Trafalgar Square this month. Cheer on runners during the **London Marathon** and celebrate **St George's Day**.

MAY

The annual **Chelsea Flower Show** blooms in May and the **May half-term** springs into action.

JUNE

Discover hidden spaces with the **Open Garden Squares Weekend**, eat well at **Taste of London**, celebrate the King's official birthday during **Trooping the Colour** and sing along at **West End LIVE** in Trafalgar Square.

JULY

Celebrate **Pride**, cheer on your favourites at **Wimbledon**, stop and smell the roses at **Hampton Court Palace Garden Festival** and have a nosy around **Buckingham Palace**, which opens to visitors this month.

AUGUST

Enjoy free art and live performances at the **Greenwich+Docklands International Festival** and get your groove on at the **Notting Hill Carnival**.

SEPTEMBER

Peek behind closed doors during **Open House London**, enjoy contemporary design with **London Design Festival**, celebrate the city's biggest river with the month-long **Totally Thames Festival** and get glammed up for **London Fashion Week**.

OCTOBER

Celebrate **Black History Month**, get arty during **Frieze London** and pull out your best costumes for **Halloween**. **October Half Term** brings family fun. **Diwali** is celebrated in Trafalgar Square.

NOVEMBER

Enjoy bonfires and fireworks for **Bonfire Night**, pay your respects on **Remembrance Day** and watch the elaborate **Lord Mayor's Show**. **Hogwarts in the Snow** opens its doors as does **Christmas at Kew** and **Winter Wonderland**.

DECEMBER

Enjoy **Christmas in London** with pantomimes, light displays, carol concerts and more. Ring in a new year with the **New Year's Eve Fireworks**.

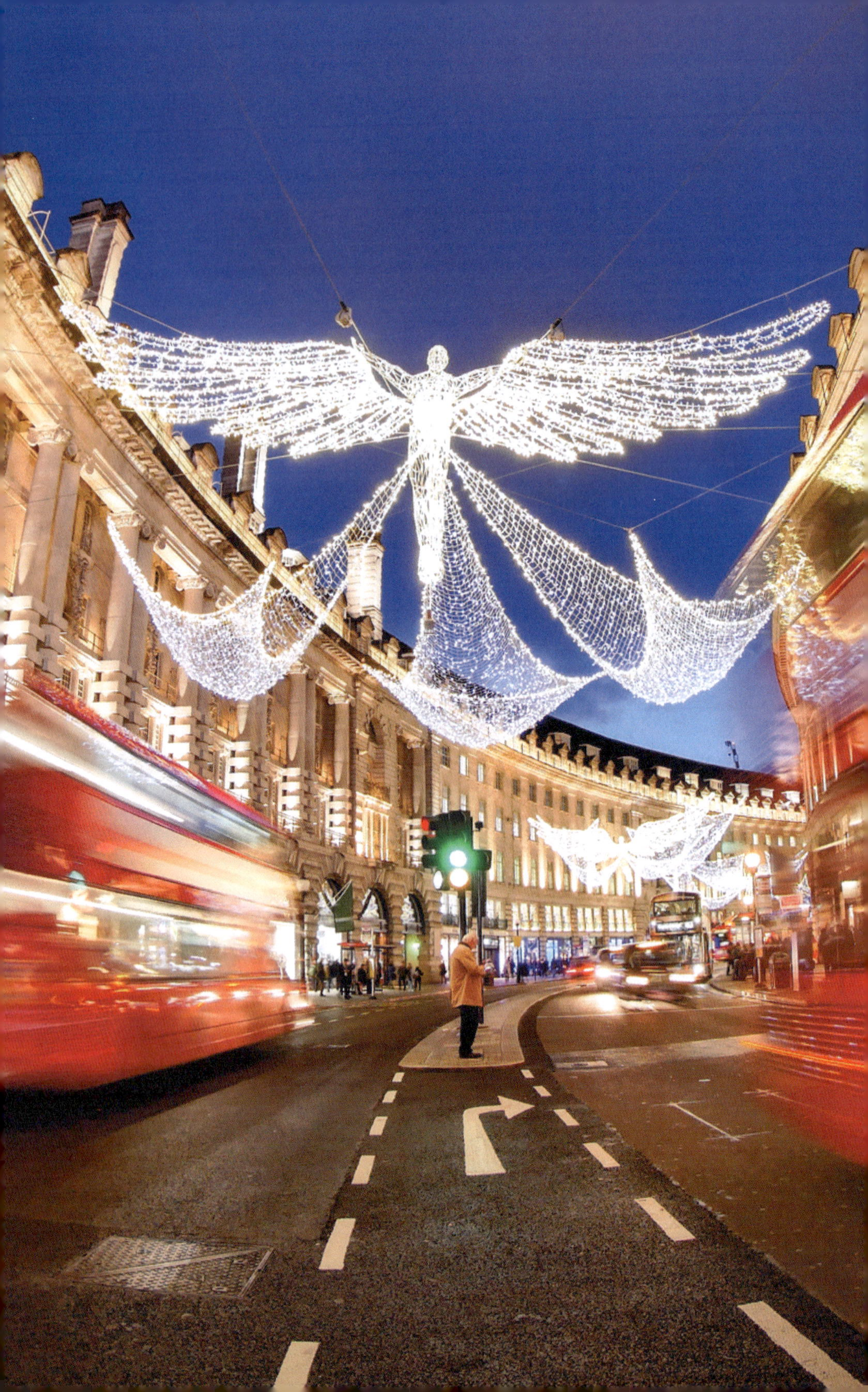

Don't leave London without...

RIDING THE TOP DECK

London's **red double-decker buses** are iconic and you get a great view from the top deck. Grab the front seats for a bird's eye view.

SPYING A RED PHONE BOX

Another London icon, these **red phone boxes** have been around since 1926 - despite attempts in the 80s to replace them. See how many you can find. Westminster is a great place to start, but expect to queue for a photo.

SNAPPING A PHOTO

You're spoiled for choice when it comes to great views of London - the blues and whites of Tower Bridge, the gothic splendour of the Houses of Parliament, the skyline seen from one of the city's skyscrapers. Or why not book a **family photoshoot** with a company like Flytographer.

BUYING A SOUVENIR

Kids will love a **Paddington Bear** from Paddington Station, or almost anything from **Hamleys**.

Be inspired by the Underground at the **London Transport Museum** shop, from the tube map on mugs to the moquette fabric from tube trains.

Fortnum & Mason is fabulous for tea and biscuits. Or browse in one of the city's great department stores such as **Liberty of London**, **Selfridges** and **Harrods**.

TRYING A BRITISH CLASSIC

It could be **fish and chips** or a good old-fashioned **Sunday roast**. Perhaps you're tempted by **afternoon tea**: an elegant classic or one with a twist. Or how about a real taste of multicultural London - **chicken tikka masala** has been called Britain's favourite dish.

Packing Checklist

CLOTHING

- [ ] One casual outfit per day
- [ ] One dressy outfit
- [ ] At least one sweater or jacket/rainjacket
- [ ] Underwear, delicates
- [ ] Socks
- [ ] Pyjamas
- [ ] Comfortable shoes/sandals/boots

TOILETRIES

- [ ] Comb/Brush
- [ ] Deodorant
- [ ] Shampoo/Conditioner
- [ ] Hairstyling products
- [ ] Soap/Face wash
- [ ] Hand sanitiser
- [ ] Toothbrush/Toothpaste/Floss
- [ ] Makeup
- [ ] Razors/Shaving cream
- [ ] Body Lotion
- [ ] Glasses/Contact lens supplies
- [ ] Personal hygiene supplies
- [ ] Sunscreen

ESSENTIALS

- [ ] Credit/Debit cards/Small amount of cash
- [ ] First aid kit (travel size)
- [ ] Camera/Video camera + Charger
- [ ] Phone/Charger
- [ ] Laptop/Charger
- [ ] Electrical converter/plug adapter
- [ ] Umbrella/Raincoat
- [ ] Rucksack/cross body bag (for everyday items)
- [ ] Sunglasses

DOCUMENTATION

- [ ] Passport/driver's licence
- [ ] Tickets (plane, train, etc)
- [ ] Itinerary
- [ ] Reservations for hotel
- [ ] Directions to hotel
- [ ] Guidebooks/maps
- [ ] This travel guide/journal

MEDICATIONS

- ☐ Painkillers
- ☐ Cold medicine/throat lozenges
- ☐ Any prescription medicine
- ☐ Allergy medications
- ☐ Diarrhoea/nausea medication

ENTERTAINMENT

- ☐ Toys
- ☐ Notebook/Pens
- ☐ Books
- ☐ Handheld electronic games
- ☐ Travel board games/cards
- ☐ Colouring/Pencil/Washable markers
- ☐ I Spy London/Activity books/London with Kids Scavenger Hunts

Essential Numbers

DOCTORS

- For everyday ailments, visit your nearest pharmacy (major chains include Boots/Superdrug)
- For non-emergency advice, dial 111
- For emergency assistance, dial 999 for an ambulance

EMERGENCY SERVICES

- **999** and **112** is the national emergency response service in the UK
- Your hotel should also be able to give advice.
- Always travel with insurance for emergencies.

GET MORE

Find more inspiration for your London trip!

Join our weekly email list to keep up with the latest London tips, attractions, new restaurant openings, holiday events and family fun, only at **facebook.com/groups/LondonwithKids**

Check out the London with Kids shop for more ways to inspire your kids or help to plan your trip.

You'll find everything from scavenger hunts and mini guides right up to our consultation service, to help tailor your itinerary to create the perfect family city break.

Go to **ko-fi.com/londonwithkids/shop** or scan the QR code below

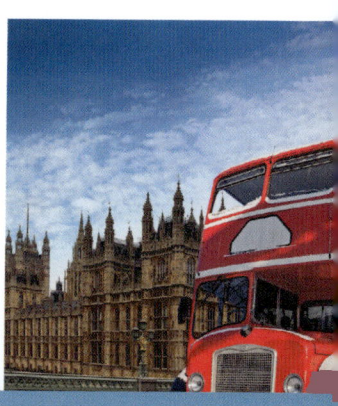

Copyright © 2025 by Katja Gaskell and Cathy Winston
All rights reserved.

No portion of this book may be reproduced in any form without written permission from the publisher or author, except as permitted by UK copyright law.

To request permission, contact the authors at hello@londonwithkids.co.uk

This publication is designed to provide accurate and authoritative information in regard to the subject matter covered. While the publisher and author have used their best efforts in preparing this book, they make no representations or warranties with respect to the accuracy or completeness of the contents of this book and specifically disclaim any implied warranties of merchantability or fitness for a particular purpose.

No warranty may be created or extended by sales representatives or written sales materials. The advice and strategies contained herein may not be suitable for your situation. You should consult with a professional when appropriate.

Neither the publisher nor the author shall be liable for any loss of profit or any other commercial damages, including but not limited to special, incidental, consequential, personal, or other damages.

Book Cover by Keryn Means Walking On Media LLC

Image credits as follows:

P4-5: Teddy bear – annbkk.gmail.com/Depositphotos
P6: Tower Bridge - irstone/Depositphotos
P7: money/models- maglara/Depositphotos; Covent Garden - rixipix/Depositphotos; view - ingus.kruklitis@gmail.com/Depositphotos
P8: Phone box - progat/Depositphotos; suitcase - tomert/Depositphotos; afternoon tea - RuthBlack/Depositphotos; feet in bed - OlegTroino/Depositphotos
P10-11: Map - dikobrazik/Depositphotos
P22: Elizabeth Tower - samot/Depositphotos
P23: Tower Bridge – kbarzycki/Depositphotos
P25: Tower of London - ArturSniezhyn/Depositphotos
P28: Natural History Museum - Jan Kranendonk/Depositphotos
P31: Neal's Yard, Covent Garden – m_ting/Depositphotos
P34: South Bank - samot/Depositphotos
P37: Greenwich - Leonid_Andronov/Depositphotos
P42: Trafalgar Square - davidewingphoto/Depositphotos
P43: Guards – SergeBertasiusPhotography/Depositphotos

Published by Katja Gaskell and Cathy Winston, www.londonwithkids.co.uk
First edition 2025.

P46: Carnaby Street - william87/Depositphotos; Selfridges - kyrien/Depositphotos; London heart - nito103/Depositphotos; Harrods - kikujungboy/Depositphotos
P49: Paddington - copyright Cathy Winston; Little Venice - encrier/Depositphotos; Portobello Road - chrisdorney/Depositphotos
P52: Monument- santirf/Depositphotos
P56: Tennis court - paulmaguire/Depositphotos
P58: Arcelor Mittal slide - chrisdorney/Depositphotos
P61: Luggage trolley - ingus.kruklitis.gmail.com/Depositphotos; Leadenhall Market & Piccadilly Circus - marcorubino/Depositphotos
P64: Buckingham Palace - pajor.pawel/Depositphotos
P65: St Paul's - zefart/Depositphotos
P70: Brighton Beach - mgphoto/Depositphotos
P71: Stonehenge - TheWalker/Depositphotos
P74: Oxford - bloodua/Depositphotos; Cambridge - godam07/Depositphotos; Hampton Court - alexey.fedoren@gmail.com/Depositphotos; Bath - antb/Depositphotos
P76: London Eye - pajor.pawel/Depositphotos
P77: Tower Bridge - photocreo/Depositphotos
P82: St James's Park – palliki/Depositphotos
P83: London pub - luckyphotographer/Depositphotos
P88: Trafalgar Square – lunamarina/Depositphotos
P89: Notting Hill houses - Baloncici/Depositphotos
P96: Underground platform - dutourdumonde/Depositphotos
P97: Trooping the Colour - magann/Depositphotos
P100: Christmas lights - joekasemsarn.gmail.com/Depositphotos
P105: London bus model - nito103/Depositphotos
P106: Elizabeth Tower - samot/Depositphotos; phone box - BrianAJackson/Depositphotos; bus - mot1963/Depositphotos

Published by Katja Gaskell and Cathy Winston, www.londonwithkids.co.uk
First edition 2025.

Printed in Dunstable, United Kingdom